VENEZUELA
in Pictures

Wendy Aalgaard

Lerner Publications Company

Contents

Lerner Publications Company
A division of Lerner Publishing Group
241 First Avenue North
Minneapolis, MN 55401 U.S.A.

Website address: www.lernerbooks.com

web enhanced @ www.vgsbooks.com

Library of Congress Cataloging-in-Publication Data

Aalgaard, Wendy, 1977-
        Venezuela in pictures / by Wendy Aalgaard.—Rev. & expanded ed.
            p.   cm. — (Visual geography series)
        Includes bibliographical references and index.
        Contents: The land—History and government—The people—Cultural life—The economy.
        ISBN: 0-8225-1172-X (lib. bdg. : alk. paper)
        1. Venezuela—Juvenile literature. [1. Venezuela.] I. Title. II. Series: Visual geography series
    (Minneapolis, Minn.)
    F2308.5.A35 2005
    987'.022'2—dc22   2003027286

Manufactured in the United States of America
1 2 3 4 5 6 - BP - 10 09 08 07 06 05

INTRODUCTION

With its majestic waterfalls, sandy beaches, golden plains, dense rain forests, and exotic wildlife, the Bolivarian Republic of Venezuela—more commonly known as Venezuela—boasts one of the most diverse ecosystems in the world. Venezuela's natural resources, particularly its petroleum deposits, also make it one of the wealthiest nations in South America.

Much of the landscape has changed since the earliest inhabitants, or indigenous groups, farmed, hunted, and roamed the region that would become Venezuela. Shortly after 1498, when Columbus set foot on the South American mainland for the first time, other explorers began seeking the riches of Venezuela. Pearls drew early settlers to the islands near Venezuela, and enslaved indigenous people brought settlers to the mainland. The newcomers exploited the region for everything it had.

Spain ruled much of the South American continent at the time. But Spain didn't take much interest in Venezuela until cacao (seeds used

to make chocolate) became the region's major cash crop in the seventeenth century. Independence came to Venezuela in 1811 under the leadership of Simón Bolívar. A series of military dictatorships governed until the mid-1900s, when Venezuela's first truly democratic government was established and more social freedoms were granted.

Oil became the focus of the economy soon after Venezuela's first commercial oil drilling in 1917. By 1926 petroleum had replaced coffee, the major cash crop of the early 1800s, as Venezuela's principal export. Abuse of power and position to gain oil profits became widespread. Government corruption did not stop, even in 1976, when Venezuela nationalized (converted from private to government ownership) all of its oil fields. Most of the oil profits were in the hands of Venezuela's wealthiest citizens. Other segments of society didn't share much in the benefits of oil.

Venezuela's position of power in the international oil market remains a core issue in Venezuelan and international affairs.

Fluctuating oil prices in world markets have created extreme highs and lows in Venezuela's economy. At the beginning of the twenty-first century, Venezuela was one of the top ten oil producers and exporters in the world, yet little of the wealth reaches the lower classes. In a land of boundless natural beauty, most Venezuelans live in extreme poverty.

The international community has also been watching Venezuela's precarious political situation. Strikes and protests have erupted against and in support of the presidency of Hugo Chávez. He promised that the oil wealth of the country would someday belong to all Venezuelans. These strikes have greatly damaged the country's economy and foreign relations. Venezuelans remain divided over their government and struggle with the economic and social future of their country.

While political and economic problems have gained Venezuela the most international attention in the beginning of the twenty-first century, little attention has been paid to Venezuela's vibrant culture. The capital city, Caracas, has always been famed for its clubs, museums, and fast-paced lifestyle. The country has also produced musicians, artists, and writers that match the genius of any of its better known Latin American neighbors. Venezuela's *telenovelas*, or soap operas, are watched all over the world. Venezuelans look forward to the day when their country will attract attention for its culture and natural beauty in addition to its petroleum wealth.

THE LAND

Venezuela is located on the northern coast of South America and has a 1,747-mile (2,813-kilometer) coastline along the Caribbean Sea and the Atlantic Ocean. To the west lies Colombia, with which Venezuela shares its early history as a nation. To the south lies Portuguese-speaking Brazil. Guyana, a former British colony, shares Venezuela's eastern border.

With 352,144 square miles (912,050 square km) of territory, Venezuela is larger than the states of Texas and Oklahoma combined. From north to south, Venezuela stretches nearly 800 miles (1,300 km). From west to east, it measures more than 900 miles (1,400 km). Four main geographical regions—the coast, the mountains, the Llanos, and the Guiana Highlands—make up mainland Venezuela. Seventy-two islands off the Caribbean coast are also Venezuelan territory.

Topography

The coast, a narrow strip of land between the mountains and the sea, is the smallest geographical region in Venezuela. The land broadens

toward the west to form the Lake Maracaibo Basin. Far to the east, the land flattens into the Orinoco Delta, the low triangular area of land where the Orinoco River branches into channels before reaching the Atlantic Ocean. Although the attractive Venezuelan islands of Los Roques, La Tortuga, and Margarita are not far off the coast, their topography differs from the rest of the region.

Lake Maracaibo in northwestern Venezuela is the main feature of the coastal region. The lake is approximately 72 miles (116 km) wide and 133 miles (214 km) long, making it the largest lake in South America. A 34-mile-wide (55-km) channel connects it with the Gulf of Venezuela. The lake lies in hot, humid lowlands encircled by the mountains of the Sierra de Perijá, the Cordillera de Mérida, and the Segovia Highlands.

The mountains of Venezuela include extensions of the Andes Mountains, the longest mountain chain in the world. The Venezuelan ranges extend in an arc from Colombia to the tip of the Paria Peninsula along the Caribbean coastline.

LAKE OF OIL

Venezuela's significant petroleum supply comes from Lake Maracaibo. Its tremendous petroleum wealth developed from mud deposits that have settled over millions of years and that are still being deposited at the bottom of the lake. Under most conditions, the lake would have filled up with sediment long ago. In fact, the channel that connects Lake Maracaibo (*above*) with the Gulf of Venezuela became so shallow that it had to be deepened to make way for oil tankers. In the rest of the lake, however, a remarkable geological process is at work. The lake bed gradually sinks at the same speed at which the sediment is deposited. Centuries of sinkage and sedimentation have formed a layer of petroleum at the bottom of the lake. From this layer, millions of barrels of oil are extracted each year.

A plant known as the **water lentil** is quickly polluting Lake Maracaibo. In early 2004, Venezuela declared a state of emergency regarding the fast-spreading plant that is threatening the fishing industry of the lake.

The Sierra de Perijá marks the Colombian border, and its slopes form the western limits of the Lake Maracaibo Basin. The highest point in the Venezuelan Andes is Pico Bolívar at 16,427 feet (5,007 meters). Pico Bolívar is part of the Cordillera de Mérida, an Andean continuation that extends for 300 miles (483 km) north to south. The Cordillera de Venezuela runs along the central Caribbean coastal region of Venezuela. Venezuela's largest cities are located on the slopes of its several mountain chains. The highlands break and continue near the Araya and Paria peninsulas.

Farther inland are more mountains. These interior ranges consist chiefly of rock, shale, sandstone, and limestone. The limestone creates spectacular formations, such as the Cave of the Guácharo, which was named after nocturnal (night) birds that appear only in northern South America.

ATLANTIC
OCEAN

CARIBBEAN SEA

Paraguaná
Peninsula

LOS ROQUES
ISLANDS

MARGARITA
ISLAND

Paria
Peninsula

Gulf of
Venezuela

LA TORTUGA
ISLAND

Araya
Peninsula

TRINIDAD

Gulf of
Paria

SIERRA DE PERIJA

SEGOVIA
HIGHLANDS

CORDILLERA DE
VENEZUELA

Cave of the
Guácharo

Lake
Maracaibo

Lake
Valencia

MARACAIBO LOWLANDS

CORDILLERA DE MÉRIDA

Pico Bolívar

Pico Espejo

Portuguesa River

Manapire River

Unare R.

L L A N O S

ORINOCO HEAVY OIL BELT

Orinoco River

Apure River

Guri Dam

Yuruari River

A N D E S   M T N S .

Arauca River

Meta River

Cerro
Bolívar

Caura River

Angel
Falls

Caroní River

GUYANA

Mount
Roraima

GUIANA
HIGHLANDS

GRAN
SABANA

COLOMBIA

Guaviare River

SIERRA PARIMA

Casiquiare Channel

Orinoco River

Equator

BRAZIL

Venezuela

Feet	Meters	
13124+	4000+	
9843	3000	Mountains
6582	2000	Uplands
3281	1000	
1640	500	Lowlands

Elevation

N

—— International border
▲ Mountain peak
■ Point of interest

0   200 Miles

0   200 KM

The flat, wide Llanos, or plains, region occupies more than one-third of Venezuela's territory and consist of both cleared savannas (grasslands) and untouched jungles. The plains are the result of mud and sand deposited by rivers over millions of years. Only a few mesas (flat-topped mountains), bits of scattered vegetation, and rivers, such as the Unare and the Manapire, break the landscape between the Andes and the Orinoco Delta. Attempts have failed to turn the plains from pastures for cattle into fields suited to the cultivation of rice and corn.

The Guiana Highlands is the fourth major geographical division. The largest of Venezuela's geographical divisions in size, the Guiana Highlands includes most of the land to the south and east of the Orinoco River. Still largely unexplored, the region contains hilly and sparsely settled areas.

Striking mountains mark the whole region. Dozens of rivers tumble over the edges of the mountains to create magnificent, gushing waterfalls. Most of Venezuela's one thousand rivers, including the Orinoco River, are found in this section of the country. South and east of the Orinoco is a land of strange granite masses, vast plateaus, and sheer mountains—in contrast to the extensive flatlands of the western plains. Finally, the spectacular Gran Sabana (Great Plain) comes into view. Its flat-topped mountains, or *tepuís*, rise up one after another, like flights of steps, as they reach thousands of feet into the sky.

In the southern Guiana Highlands, near Brazil, lies Venezuela's Amazon territory. The territory's thick jungles are crossed by numerous rivers, and its boundary lies less than 100 miles (161 km) from the equator.

> The arid state of Falcón, which lies north of the Cordillera de Mérida, is the only region resembling a desert in Venezuela.

◉ Rivers

The Orinoco River begins in the Sierra Parima near Brazil's border. Upstream and not far from their source, the waters of the Orinoco River divide. One-third becomes the southern Casiquiare Channel and continues to the mighty Amazon River. Strangely, the point where the division takes place—777 miles (1,250 km) from the sea by the Orinoco course and 1,864 miles (3,000 km) from the sea by the Amazon route—is only 395 feet (120 m) above sea level. In other words, the river's incline is so slight as to be inadequate for the water to flow for long distances. Seasonal rainfall—rather than the powerful runoff from melted Andean snow—causes the rivers to move. Downstream from the dividing point, the Orinoco has a 25-mile-long

The Orinoco River flows 600,000 cubic feet (182,880 m) per second, making it the eighth largest river in the world by volume.

(40 km) course of rapids, which is the only barrier to continuous navigation to the Gulf of Paria.

The Orinoco has many tributaries along its 1,300-mile (2,092-km) length. From the west, large waterways—the Guaviare, the Meta, the Arauca, the Apure, and the Portuguesa rivers—that originate in the Andes Mountains flow into the Orinoco. From the south and east, the Orinoco is enlarged by the dark waters of the Caroní and Caura rivers, which come from the mountains of the Gran Sabana and the Guiana Highlands. On approaching the Caribbean Sea, the Orinoco divides itself again and forms a delta, distributing its waters through outlets into the Atlantic Ocean.

Although the Orinoco River dominates Venezuela's waterway system, the nation also has hundreds of lakes and beautiful lagoons (shallow ponds connected to larger bodies of water). During the wet season, the rivers swell and flood the lagoons, and the lakes rise so high that the overflowing waters threaten nearby cities.

Angel Falls

Angel Falls, the highest waterfall in the world, is located on an upper tributary of the Caroní River. The total drop of 3,212 feet (979 m) is more than fifteen times longer than the descent of Niagara Falls.

Unlike other waterfalls, Angel Falls does not flow over the top of a cliff. The water gathers underground and erupts from several crevices located 300 feet (91 m) below the top of a huge flat-topped mountain named Auyán-tepuí. The area is often subject to fierce thunderstorms and mysterious cloud formations, which frequently hide the falls from view. Although the site has been a popular tourist attraction ever since its discovery, it was not until 1971 that anyone succeeded in scaling the steep sides to reach its top.

Angel Falls was first observed from the air in 1935 by a pilot named Jimmy Angel. He was exploring the mystery of El Dorado (the golden one)—a legendary treasure of gold said to be hidden in the area. Although the falls would later bear Angel's name, the Pemón Indians had already given the site of Angel Falls, with its deadly drop, a different name—Auyán-tepuí, or Devil's Mountain.

◎ Climate

Venezuela's varied landscape and elevation create four distinct climatic zones. The tropical zone, or *tierra caliente*, climbs from sea level to 2,600 feet (792 m) in altitude and has temperatures ranging from 76°F to 96°F (24°C to 36°C). This zone includes the coastlines and the areas at the base of the mountains, as well as the plains, valleys, and deltas of the Orinoco River. Also located in this zone is the city of Maracaibo, with an average temperature of 83°F (28°C) and an average humidity of 77 percent, making it one of the hottest and most humid cities in South America.

The moderate zone, called the *tierra templada*, consists of the next highest levels of the mountains up to 6,500 feet (1,981 m). The area's temperatures are mild—50°F to 77°F (10°C to 25°C). The air is cool and moist at higher elevations, but at lower elevations, it can often be hot and humid.

The cool zone, or *tierra fría*, found only in the mountainous areas above 6,500 feet (1,981 m), has temperatures ranging between 34°F and 75°F (1°C and 24°C). Above the tierra fría in the Andean Cordillera de Mérida is the *páramos* region, where the snow never melts. This region is much colder than the cool zone, and the average year-round temperature is 17°F (−8°C).

Rainfall varies a great deal from region to region. Despite Maracaibo's high humidity, the city gets only about 23 inches (58 centimeters) of precipitation in an average year. Further east on the Caribbean coast, the capital city of Caracas averages 32 inches (81 cm) each year, while Ciudad Bolívar along the Orinoco River receives 41 inches (104 cm) or more. In December 1999, extremely heavy rains caused flash floods and subsequent mudslides along the coast, devastating towns around Caracas and La Guaira and killing more than thirty thousand people.

The Llanos region usually experiences the most extreme rainy and dry seasons. During the rainy season, from May to November, heavy rains fall, and the swollen rivers flood large stretches of land. Travel by land is difficult or impossible except on the main highways. In the dry season, from December through April, many of the rivers dry up and pastures wither. Cattle find little to feed on, and even the tropical rain forest loses some of its foliage.

Flora and Fauna

Due to its varied weather and elevation, Venezuela boasts one of the most diverse ecosystems in the world. The majority of Venezuela's plant and animal life inhabits the jungles and savannas. Rain forests cover about half of Venezuela and feature stands of brazilwood and coral trees, as well as trees and shrubs that produce tropical fruits, such as mangoes and papayas. Howler and spider monkeys sit in the trees, and formidable boa and anaconda snakes slither across the forest floor.

The endless savanna, beautified by miriti palm trees, provides homes for gorgeous, colorful birds. *Chenchenas* (small herons), scarlet ibis, and troupials fly overhead. Anteaters, capybaras (large web-footed rodents that are also called *chigüires*), jaguars, and peccaries (wild pigs) roam the land.

The scarlet ibis inhabits the rich grasslands of the Llanos.

Weighing nearly 140 pounds (64 kilograms) and standing nearly 2 feet (0.6 m) tall, web-footed **capybaras** are eaten by many Venezuelans during the Easter season. To find links for more information about the capybara and other Venezuelan animals, visit www.vgsbooks.com.

WHEN RODENTS RULED

Already home to the capybara, the world's largest rodent, Venezuela was apparently once the land of the largest rodent that ever lived. *Phoberomys pattersoni* (foh-BAIR-oh-mihs pat-ur-SOH-nee), as it was named, probably lived eight million years ago. Its fossils were discovered in Venezuela in 1999. Unlike the measly 140-pound (64 kg) capybara, this ancient rodent was estimated to weigh 1,500 pounds (700 kg) and was 9 feet (2.7 m) long. That's one big rodent!

The Caribbean Sea and Venezuela's many rivers and lakes are home to a variety of living creatures. Crocodiles, including the endangered Orinoco crocodile, hunt the waterways and lagoons of overflowing rivers. The Orinoco River contains electric eels that can paralyze a bull with their electrical charges and ferocious piranhas that can eat an animal in a matter of seconds. The river's edible bagres (catfish) can grow over 4 feet (1.2 m) long and weigh up to 200 pounds (91 kg). Manatees and freshwater dolphins also swim in the warm Orinoco waters. When the Orinoco's tributaries overflow every year, the river creatures coexist with the inhabitants of the Llanos. Pastureland becomes lakes, cattle drink from the same water where piranhas swim, and thousands of birds flock to the region.

The tepuís of the Gran Sabana are home to truly unique plant and animal life. These large plateaus, peeking out through heavy cloud cover, have virtually no soil. Nevertheless, orchids and carnivorous plants cling to the rock. Each tepuí is its own ecosystem because the steep sides make it difficult for new animals to climb them. Unlike other parts of the country, where nonnative plant and animal species have been introduced over the years, many tepuí plant species have been evolving for millions of years.

Canaima National Park holds more than 550 species of birds and an estimated 500 species of orchids.

To protect the spectacular plants, animals, and geological formations of the Venezuelan landscape, the country has set aside nearly 15 percent of its land as national parks. Of the more than forty parks in Venezuela, the most well known is Canaima National Park, which lies in the Gran Sabana and is home to Angel Falls and the tepuís.

Natural Resources

Hidden in the magnificent Venezuelan landscape is an abundance of natural resources. The most significant—petroleum—was discovered in the early 1900s. Its discovery would forever change Venezuela. The country's largest petroleum supply comes from the Maracaibo Lowlands, specifically Lake Maracaibo. Millions of barrels of oil are extracted from the bottom of the lake each year.

Along the northern shore of the Orinoco River in the Llanos, lies the Orinoco Heavy Oil Belt, a vast expanse of petroleum deposits. These deposits, which are said to rival those of the oil superpower, Saudi Arabia, have remained undeveloped because the oil is difficult to extract. In the late 1980s, the Venezuelan government formed a company to exploit these reserves. The southern shore of the Orinoco has gold, iron ore, diamonds, and bauxite.

The Guiana Highlands contain hilly areas that are rich in forest and mineral resources. The rain forests provide timber resources and hold invaluable medicinal plants. The mountains consist of rock overlaid with sandstone and volcanic deposits. The mineral deposits that the highlands contain have never been fully tapped. The search for diamonds is often successful, although devastating to the land and indigenous people. Gold has also lured prospectors to the Guiana Highlands for decades. Farther south, beyond lowlands and jungles crossed by many rivers, is the Yuruari River, which is also rich in gold. The most important mineral resource of the Guiana Highlands is iron ore. Sandstone-covered granite with a high content of pure iron makes up the Cerro Bolívar and the Llanos city of El Pao in Bolívar State.

Water from Venezuela's rivers provides important energy resources. The Caroní River is harnessed by the Guri Dam, which produces more than ten million megawatts of power a day for Venezuela and parts of Colombia. This is not enough to power Venezuela's growing energy needs, however, and power outages are a frequent problem.

The Environment

Although the sparsely populated regions of the country remain relatively untouched, efforts to access Venezuela's abundant natural resources have caused serious environmental problems. Mining, heavy deforestation (tree removal), and massive urban growth have taken their

Deforestation has taken its toll on Venezuela's environment. To learn more about what is being done to prevent deforestation, visit www.vgsbooks.com.

Small-scale oil leaks, such as this one, may not seem like a big deal, but even a tiny leak can kill wildlife and ruin ecosystems.

toll on the countryside. The oil rigs in Lake Maracaibo create pollution in the Maracaibo Lowlands.

Numerous indigenous groups live in Amazonas State in southern Venezuela. Although their homelands are protected by law from most outsiders (scientists and missionaries are often granted special permission), little has been done to stop encroaching miners and poachers. President Hugo Chávez encouraged indigenous groups to stake legal claims to their land before it is destroyed. Attempts have been made to rectify some environmental concerns, but the current economic and political unrest of the nation is more of a priority for most Venezuelans.

Major Cities

Recent years have witnessed a rapid movement of the rural population to cities and towns. About 87 percent of Venezuela's total population lives in urban areas, such as Caracas, with most of the nation's people concentrated in cities and towns near the coast or within Venezuela's mountain chains. Migration from city to city is also becoming more commonplace, as residents of large cities move to medium-sized cities, such as Valencia, to find a better standard of living. In contrast to the coast and the Cordillera de Venezuela, the Llanos, the Lake Maracaibo Basin, and the Guiana Highlands are sparsely settled.

CARACAS, the capital of Venezuela, is in a narrow valley bordered by steep mountains, 3,000 feet (914 m) above sea level. In the last several decades,

The towering high-rises and congested highways of **Caracas** sprawl in the valley beneath the wooded slopes of Avila Mountain. Since World War II (1939–1945), Caracas has increased in size and population faster than any other Latin American city.

Caracas has changed dramatically from a provincial city to one of the richest and most modern capitals in the world. Many of its colonial structures have been replaced with tall apartment and office buildings. Its old dirt roads have been paved over by an *autopista*—a system of superhighways.

The city has a population of over 2 million, but the larger metropolitan area has approximately 5 to 6 million people—about twenty times its population in 1941. Growth has resulted in traffic jams on the autopista—only partially relieved by a subway system. Housing is insufficient, so many poor people have built shacks, called *ranchos,* on the city's surrounding hills, which are too steep for conventional construction. These communities of temporary housing are known as barrios and often lack essential services, such as running water and proper waste management.

Caracas is rich in history and culture, however. The birthplace of Simón Bolívar—one of Venezuela's most famous sons—is within the city limits, as are many interesting museums, churches, and public buildings.

MARACAIBO rivals Caracas in size but owes its importance to the oil industry that developed just beyond its shores in Lake Maracaibo. The city has become a thriving industrial and commercial hub of about 2 million people.

VALENCIA (population 1.4 million) lies in the middle of the leading agricultural region in northern Venezuela and is the country's most industrialized city. In 1830 Valencia was briefly the nation's capital, but disease-breeding marshes between the city and nearby Lake Valencia discouraged early settlers. At the beginning of the twenty-first century, Valencia has become one of Venezuela's fastest growing cities.

◉ Secondary Cities

Barquisimeto, a large city with about 900,000 inhabitants, lies in good livestock-grazing country. Rebuilt completely after an earthquake in 1812, Barquisimeto is a commercial center located on the Pan-American Highway (the highway system running from western Alaska to western Chile) about 150 miles (241 km) from the Caribbean Sea.

At the junction of the Orinoco and Caroní rivers is Ciudad Guayana—the industrial capital of Venezuela's iron and steel belt. The city was built to attract residents of large cities, such as Caracas, into the interior regions of the country. From a small village in 1960, Ciudad Guayana has grown into a bustling metropolis of more than 700,000 people.

Until surpassed in size by Ciudad Guayana, Ciudad Bolívar (population 300,000) on the Orinoco River was the largest inland city in Venezuela. When Simón Bolívar headed Venezuela in the 1820s, Ciudad Bolívar, then named Angostura (narrows), was the capital of the eastern plains, the Orinoco Delta region, and the Guiana Highlands.

Visit www.vgsbooks.com for links to websites with additional information about the many things to see and do in Venezuela's cities, as well as links to websites about Venezuela's weather, natural resources, plants and animals, and more.

HISTORY AND GOVERNMENT

Christopher Columbus landed in Venezuela on August 1, 1498, during his third voyage to the New World. After reaching the island of Trinidad, he sailed along the coast toward the west and saw land that he mistook for another island. He named the area Isla de Gracía (Isle of Grace). Columbus first set foot on the South American continent on Venezuelan soil.

Columbus was not the first person in the region, however. Venezuela's indigenous people had farmed, hunted, fished, and roamed the area for nearly sixteen thousand years. Besides the Arhuaco and the Wayúu (Guajíra), there were the Caribs—a warlike people who had spread to the farthest corners of the territory. The Betoya and Timote lived in the Cordillera de Mérida and were believed to be descendants of the Chibcha Indians of Colombia.

The name Venezuela, which means "Little Venice," appeared for the first time shortly after Columbus's arrival. In 1499 another explorer, Alonso de Ojeda, sailed along the northern coast of South

America as far as Lake Maracaibo. He saw indigenous peoples living in groups of houses built on stilts over the waters of the lake. These dwellings reminded him of the Italian lagoon city of Venezia, or Venice.

Conquest of Venezuela

Many Spaniards followed Columbus to South America in search of gold and other riches rumored to be found in the region. At the beginning of the sixteenth century, the earliest known Spanish settlement, Nueva Cádiz, was established in the northeastern part of Venezuela on Cubagua Island. The inhabitants of the territory fiercely resisted the foreign settlements, but the Spaniards were determined to conquer the area, which was rich in pearls. They sent expedition after expedition to subdue the local groups. Before the end of the sixteenth century, the conquistadors (Spanish explorers who conquered lands in Central and South America) had established settlements at Cumaná, Coro, El

HENRY MORGAN AND THE SIEGE OF MARACAIBO

Pirates eventually replaced indigenous groups as the source of early colonial concern. The Caribbean coast of Venezuela and the large settlements of Caracas and Maracaibo were favorite points of pirate attacks. Sir Francis Drake, an English adventurer, took pleasure in plundering Spanish towns and sacked Caracas in 1585.

Perhaps the most famous attack on Venezuela was the siege of Maracaibo. In 1669 Henry Morgan—a Welsh buccaneer who operated from the island of Jamaica—entered Lake Maracaibo from the Gulf of Venezuela. Upon arriving at Maracaibo, Morgan found the city seemingly undefended and collected a large booty. When the pirate turned his ships to exit the lake, he found himself and his fleet looking into the guns of three Spanish warships. Craftily, Morgan used one of his pirate boats as a decoy. After the decoy was set on fire, it was launched into the middle of the Spanish ships and managed to sink two of the war vessels. Once free of the danger of Spanish guns, Morgan made his escape.

Tocuyo, Barquisimeto, Valencia, Mérida, Trujillo, Caracas, and La Guaira.

Coro became important because of its business and political activities, especially after 1528, when representatives of a German banking firm set up headquarters in the town. The newly chosen Holy Roman emperor, Charles V, or King Charles I of Spain, granted rights to this company to exploit the wealth of western Venezuela. In so doing, Charles V paid off his debt to the German firm, from whom he had borrowed heavily in his bid for the imperial crown.

Unsure of how long its rights would last, the company looted the colony and slaughtered many of the native inhabitants. Two adventurers who worked as representatives for the company were especially notorious—Ambrosio Alfinger and Nicholas Federmann. These men so abused their contract that Spain finally ended its agreement with the banking firm. The Spaniards, thereafter, undertook to colonize Venezuela themselves.

The Spanish found that conquering Venezuela was not a simple task. The tough and able leader of the Teques Indians, Guaicaipuro, organized a huge warrior force that attacked early Spanish settlements, causing many of them to be abandoned. Although the Spaniards encountered few pockets of resistance in the coastal areas, they did not subdue the central portion of the colony until after the death of Guaicaipuro in the mid-1500s.

◉ Colonial Era

For many years, Spain was the dominant power in Central and South America and controlled its New World empire mainly from Lima, the capital of present-day Peru. As part of the Spanish system of governing, Spain established an *audiencia,* or administrative center, in Santo Domingo on the island of Hispaniola (shared by modern-day Haiti and the Dominican Republic). In 1526 Venezuela's territory came under the authority of the Audiencia of Santo Domingo. In 1550 Venezuela was combined with the territory of present-day Colombia to form the Audiencia of Santa Fe de Bogotá. In 1718 this same area was added to what is modern Ecuador to form the Viceroyalty of New Granada, though Venezuela was still governed by Spain. Finally, in 1777, the provinces of Caracas, Maracaibo, Barinas, Cumaná, and the islands of Margarita and Trinidad were merged into a captaincy general (military governorship) in Venezuela. Limited governing power eventually came to the colony in 1786, when Spain created the Audiencia of Caracas.

The Spanish attitude toward all of its New World colonies was to exploit the natural wealth of the region and force the native groups into slave labor. Spanish settlers eventually grew valuable agricultural products, such as cacao and tobacco. Venezuelans began trading heavily with British, French, and Dutch traders. African slaves were imported and traded to work on agricultural estates.

The Spanish considered Venezuela's trade with other countries to be illegal. The Royal Guipúzcoana Company of Caracas, better known as the Caracas Company, was granted a monopoly on all trade within the colony. The company created wealth and developed

CLASS SYSTEM

After the conquest of Venezuela, the population of the territory divided into three classes. At the top of the social and economic ladder were the Spanish-born people, who held the reins of government and enjoyed the privileges of their offices. Next in order came the Venezuelan-born descendants of the Spanish—known as criollos (Creoles). The richest class by virtue of its landholdings, this class was frustrated in its hopes to govern its own country. At the bottom were people of mixed racial backgrounds (called pardos or mestizos), indigenous people, and Africans, who had originally been brought as slaves to work the land.

agriculture. Consequently, exports to Spain increased. But the cost of this record of achievement—low wages for Venezuelan workers and high prices for all imported goods—sowed the seeds of discontent that eventually led to revolution and independence.

Independence

By the late eighteenth century, dissatisfied Venezuelans became increasingly agitated against Spain, whose methods of exploitation slowed economic development in the area. An independence movement began that included both the poor, overworked native groups and the wealthy Creoles. The ideas of democracy and the successful wars of independence in the United States and France influenced these anticolonials.

The Spanish crown, on the other hand, felt that Venezuela should continue to be controlled by officials sent from Spain. Friction with the Creoles resulted in revolutionary movements in several parts of Venezuela. At first, the Spanish authorities quickly put down such rebellions, but the independence movement could not be halted for very long after the beginning of the nineteenth century.

Caracas-born Francisco de Miranda was one of the most important figures in Venezuela's struggle for independence. He is known in Venezuela as El Precursor (the Forerunner) because of his early efforts to free his native land from Spanish colonial domination. A soldier in the Spanish army, Miranda had fought in the American Revolution (1775–1783). He led a revolutionary expedition into Venezuela in 1806 but failed to accomplish his plan to liberate the colony. He went into exile in London.

April 19, 1810, marks the formal beginning of Venezuela's struggle for independence. On that date, a group of Caracas aristocrats and wealthy Creoles forced the Spanish governor from office and formed a junta, or revolutionary council, to take over the government. The junta at first described itself as loyal to the Spanish king, Ferdinand VII. But it later issued a declaration of full independence. The fight for independence went on for many years, however, and Venezuela lost nearly one-third of its population to bloodshed.

In April of 1810, Miranda returned to Venezuela and took an important position in the rebel forces that the junta had organized. Along with many other Venezuelan patriots of the period, Francisco de Miranda signed the nation's declaration of independence on July 5, 1811, in Caracas. Rebel losses led Miranda to surrender to the Spanish in 1812. The Spanish broke the terms of Miranda's surrender and deported him in chains to Spain, where he died in prison four years later.

This painting by Martín Tovar y Tovar depicts **Francisco de Miranda** signing Venezuela's declaration of independence. For links that explain more about Venezuela's independence movement, visit www.vgsbooks.com.

Simón Bolívar

Simón Bolívar outshines Miranda as the liberator not only of Venezuela but also of Colombia, Panama, Ecuador, Peru, and Bolivia. Born in Caracas in 1783, Bolívar was educated by private tutors in Venezuela and later in Spain. From his studies, the young Venezuelan absorbed the democratic ideals described by the French philosopher Jean-Jacques Rousseau. Bolívar's early association with Latin American independence was largely unsuccessful. He lost important battles in 1812 but led the rebel soldiers to many victories in the next two years. In 1817 he united his forces with those of José Antonio Páez. Thereafter, victory followed victory, and in 1819 Bolívar's long-held vision of a united South America became a partial reality as Gran Colombia (Great Colombia), a federation of what would become the nations of Ecuador, Colombia, Panama, and Venezuela. After repeated attempts to defeat the Spanish, Bolívar devised a plan to split the Spanish forces and scored a decisive victory over them in 1819.

Bolívar was elected president of Gran Colombia. In 1821 a victory at Carabobo (near Valencia) finally ensured indepen-dence for Venezuela, and Bolívar entered Caracas in triumph. But he continued

As liberator of much of South America, **Simón Bolívar** had been president in both Columbia and Peru before his brief Venezuelan presidency.

to fight for the freedom of the rest of Gran Colombia and South America.

By 1825 Bolívar had helped to free much of South America and was the most powerful man on the continent. Soon, however, opposition to his power arose, and he was nearly assassinated when he declared himself a dictator to enforce his rule. He could not halt the crumbling of Gran Colombia in 1830, and he resigned from the presidency in despair when Venezuela and Ecuador left the federation that year. Bolívar died a few months later, embittered by strife and the collapse of his political dream. It was not until much later that South Americans recognized him as one of the greatest heroes of Latin American history.

The Caudillos

After Bolívar's resignation and death, José Antonio Páez dictated Venezuela's policies both through his position as president and later through his personal influence. In 1843, when José Tadeo Monagas was elected president, Páez began a revolt against Monagas and tried to have him legally removed from office. Quick to react, however, Monagas put down the revolt and forced Páez into exile. Monagas remained in power until 1858, when he was overthrown in a surprise revolt supported by both conservative and liberal politicians. Thus began a period of 130 years during which the norm in Venezuela was either short-term rulers, who were quickly overthrown, or long-term dictators, who imposed themselves on the country through superior military strength. The most remembered leaders of this period were the caudillos (tyrannical political leaders with a strong military following).

One of the early caudillos was Antonio Guzmán Blanco, who took power in 1870. Guzmán Blanco ruled Venezuela for the next eighteen years and is considered an example of a benevolent, if self-serving, tyrant.

During his lengthy reign, he oversaw the beginning of a system of compulsory public education, slightly reformed the operations of the government, and undertook much public construction. Guzmán Blanco also commissioned many paintings and statues of himself.

Guzmán Blanco never legally served as president during all of the eighteen years he ran Venezuela. In 1888 one of his puppets, Joaquín Crespo, overthrew Guzmán Blanco to make himself dictator. In 1899 a new dictator—General Cipriano Castro—replaced Crespo.

The Twentieth Century

Corrupt, greedy, and incompetent, Castro soon had the nation's finances in chaos and refused to honor Venezuela's financial obligations to foreign creditors. In 1902 Great Britain, Germany, and Italy sent a joint naval force to blockade and shell Venezuelan seaports as a means of collecting Venezuela's unpaid foreign debts. The U.S. military intervened to end foreign interference in the Western Hemisphere, and Castro agreed to take care of the debts.

Castro was followed by Juan Vicente Gómez—one of the longest lasting of all Latin American dictators. Gómez ruled Venezuela as an absolute dictator from 1908 until his death in 1935. To staff his repressive government, Gómez relied on relatives and trusted friends from Táchira, his rugged, Andean home state. To keep himself in power, Gómez modernized the army and constantly rotated its top commanders to prevent any one officer from becoming powerful enough to challenge his authority.

BORDER DISPUTE

During Crespo's regime, a Venezuelan boundary dispute attracted international attention. Great Britain and Venezuela had a long-standing disagreement over where the boundary between Venezuela and the colony of British Guiana (present-day Guyana) should be drawn.

In 1895 the United States demanded that Great Britain allow the matter to go to international resolution. Lord Salisbury, the British prime minister, politely refused, which angered U.S. president Grover Cleveland. Cleveland took the matter to the U.S. Congress, where he denounced Britain's unwillingness to cooperate.

With talk of a possible war, which neither the United States nor Britain wanted, Britain allowed the dispute to be resolved by international efforts. In 1899 the new boundary line was drawn in favor of Britain. But the Venezuelan government still claims much of the area west of the Essequibo River as part of Venezuela.

"BLACK GOLD"

Before Venezuela's oil boom in the 1920s, the country was predominantly agricultural. For four hundred years, it depended on earnings from exports of coffee, cacao, animal hides, fruits, sisal (a strong fiber used in rope making), and gold. Venezuela purchased from foreign markets almost every manufactured product that Venezuelans used.

Then, when oil was discovered in great quantities beneath the surface of Lake Maracaibo, a rapid change took place. European and U.S. companies sent people to Venezuela to drill and process the newly found petroleum. Gasoline-driven cars had become commonplace in most industrial countries. The demand for oil rose quickly and brought vast wealth to Venezuela.

But the wealth went into the pockets of foreign investors and corrupt Venezuelan government officials. Little trickled down to the Venezuelan people. As demand for oil grew and as new deposits were found, oil became the only real industry in Venezuela, weakening agriculture.

In the early 1900s, oil was discovered in Lake Maracaibo, and Venezuela's oil industry began. Gómez had the good fortune to rule Venezuela when foreign oil companies were lining up to obtain lucrative concessions (rights) from the nation's oil bonanza. Foreign companies, who had the means to obtain and refine the oil, paid Venezuela a share of their profits for the rights to take the oil. With increased revenues from oil, Gómez was able to pay off Venezuela's debts while building up his own wealth. The longer he held power, however, the more tyrannical his regime became. He ignored social issues, agriculture, and industry—except for the development of petroleum. This neglect resulted in severe hardships for most Venezuelans.

In the dictator's final years, information about the torture of Gómez's political enemies shocked Venezuela and the world. After his death in 1935, Venezuelans' anger exploded over Gómez's active role in selling the country's oil rights to foreigners. Citizens massacred Gómez-era officials and attacked oil company installations in the Lake Maracaibo area.

◉ Contemporary Democracy

Some historians date the origins of Venezuela's contemporary democracy to the death of Gómez, even though unsettled times still lay ahead. In 1935 Eleázar López Contreras was elected president for a five-year term. Though still a dictator, he loosened the grip of the Gómez-era organizations of repression. He was followed in office by Isaías Medina Angarita, who continued to stabilize Venezuelan politics. Students and political activists who had been imprisoned or exiled for speaking against the Gómez government were freed or encouraged to return home.

Among those who returned was a dynamic revolutionary leader, Rómulo Betancourt, head of the Democratic Action (AD) Party. His party was a liberal-minded group that had helped pressure the conservative government into increasing Venezuela's share of the profits of foreign-owned oil companies.

Betancourt's followers demanded far-reaching changes. These new ideas frightened both the leadership of Venezuela's conservative, influential military establishment and its foreign backers—the oil companies. In 1945, when President Medina Angarita tried to select his successor, the civilian Betancourt and some of the more liberal junior officers within the military staged a coup d'état, or government takeover.

After the coup, Betancourt headed a seven-member junta, whose stated purpose was to make sure elections were held. But the junta took advantage of its three-year tenure in office to undertake radical reforms. Government officials guilty of using their positions for personal gain under previous administrations were brought to trial. Under Juan Pablo Pérez Alfonso—Betancourt's minister of development—new taxes were imposed on foreign oil companies. As a result, the profits of the Venezuelan government rose from 30 to 50 percent.

When elections were held in 1947, Rómulo Gallegos, a novelist and candidate of Betancourt's AD Party, was elected by an overwhelming majority of the Venezuelan voters. Gallegos refused to bow to military demands for cabinet posts. Furthermore, there was growing agitation over the radical direction being taken by the leadership of the AD Party. A conservative military coup overthrew Gallegos in November 1948, only eight months after he had taken office.

A period of repressive military rule followed—including the exiling again of Betancourt, Gallegos, and many other AD members. In the 1950s, Marcos Pérez Jiménez presided over one of Venezuela's most repressive regimes. He authorized, for example, the establishment of an elaborate police network, which spied on, harassed, and imprisoned students, intellectuals, and politicians who disagreed with his policies. Besides trampling on human rights, Pérez Jiménez increased his personal wealth to $700 million until a coalition forced him from office in 1958. Later, a constitutional amendment would bar him from seeking the presidency again.

In 1956, during the regime of Marcos Pérez Jiménez, the Suez Canal was closed to the exportation of Middle Eastern oil. This act resulted in an unprecedented expansion of Venezuelan oil production and earnings.

The police network created by Pérez Jiménez made many Venezuelans unhappy. In January 1958, a large mob gathered outside police headquarters and set fire to many police cars to protest the network.

Rómulo Betancourt once again became the head of the Venezuelan government in 1959. This time, he was chosen as president in a democratic national election. A tough but immensely popular man, Betancourt supported radical leftist political views in his early years but later became a social reformer with great faith in the democratic process.

Betancourt demonstrated that overdue social changes could be brought about by democratic means. He used his growing personal popularity with the Venezuelan people to enact programs of agrarian (farming) reform and to improve standards of housing, health, and education. He developed the notion of "sowing the petroleum"—using the profits from oil to better the lives of Venezuelans. Betancourt also created new industries so that the Venezuelan economy was not solely dependent on oil. Until the end of his presidency in 1964, Betancourt faced opposition within Venezuela, both from ultra-liberal groups and from conservative sections of the military.

Betancourt's most important contribution, however, was to lay the foundations of a stable democracy in Venezuela. Since this achievement, power has alternated between the liberal AD Party and the conservative Christian Democratic, or Social Christian, Party (COPEI). By working together within the framework of democracy, these two main parties, along with smaller political parties, have provided Latin America with a rare example of democracy in action.

After Betancourt

During the last part of the twentieth century, Venezuela successfully weathered threats to its stability. In the late 1960s and early 1970s, for example, guerrilla groups tried to disrupt the country's election process through robberies, kidnappings, and threats.

Venezuela also has had to cope with continuing government corruption. Some high-ranking government officials were guilty of accepting bribes and taking part in secret commissions during the administration of Carlos Andrés Pérez, who came to power in 1974. One of his most significant acts was to switch ownership of the country's oil industry from private hands to the state—a process called nationalization. In the 1970s, when Venezuela's income from oil quadrupled, the administration had more revenue to spend from oil earnings than all previous Venezuelan administrations since independence. Much of it was spent on employment programs, but the middle and upper classes still held the most wealth.

Venezuela's encounter with extreme wealth was brief. When oil prices fell in the late 1970s, Venezuela's economy tumbled with it. In 1983 Jaime Lusinchi—an AD Party member—was elected to the Venezuelan presidency with the largest majority in twenty-five years of democracy. Lusinchi initiated measures to counter the ailing economy and to repay foreign debts.

In 1988 the people again elected Carlos Andrés Pérez president. Although Pérez had been responsible for nationalizing Venezuela's oil and iron industries, his major objective during his second administration was to open up Venezuela's markets to private ownership. Soon after taking office, Pérez raised prices on items such as gasoline and public transportation. These efforts to improve Venezuela's economy provoked rioting. To restore peace, Pérez froze prices on some items and raised wages.

Criticism of government policies and charges of corruption continued to plague the president. National strikes and demonstrations took place. The Bolívar Revolutionary Movement staged two unsuccessful government overthrows. The Venezuelan legislature forced Pérez from office in May 1993 on charges of corruption and the misuse of public funds.

Interim president Ramón José Velásquez contended with a sluggish economy and a widening budget deficit before turning over the office to Rafael Caldera in February 1994. Caldera vowed to continue government control of the business sector. In the months following Caldera's inauguration, bankruptcies rose dramatically and the banking system collapsed. President Caldera eventually accepted assistance from the International Monetary Fund (IMF), a UN agency that provides short-term credit. But part of the deal involved lifting price controls and laying off thousands of public workers. Unemployment rose, and inflation exploded to 103 percent.

The Bolivarian Republic of Venezuela

In 1998 Hugo Chávez Frías was elected president of Venezuela. Chávez was a former paratrooper and one of the leaders of the Bolívar Revolutionary Movement. With his background as a working-class citizen and his ties to the military, Chávez was elected by 56 percent of the vote. As one of his first acts as president, he renamed the country the Bolivarian Republic of Venezuela to commemorate Simón Bolívar and his revolution. Chávez also appointed a committee to rewrite the country's constitution. The new constitution was intended to rid the government of corruption and to improve the lives of the working class and indigenous peoples. Promises to redistribute the wealth of the country gained him strong supporters among these groups. But his authoritarian control of the government and the threat of a working-class uprising made him many enemies, especially among the middle and upper classes. Violent protests both for and against Chávez's government plagued the country's major cities in the early twenty-first century.

The problems of Chávez's presidency extend to foreign relations as well. Chávez outraged many nations—most significantly the United States, a key trading partner—when he maintained relations with dictators such as Saddam Hussein of Iraq and Fidel Castro of Cuba.

An attempted coup in 2002 removed Chávez from power for a day before he was back in power. At the end of 2002, a nationwide strike of workers at the government-run petroleum plant halted economic activity. The strike ended with opposing sides signing an agreement.

Ironically, the 1999 constitution that Chávez initiated gives voters the power to recall the president in a referendum, or direct vote, after the president has completed half a term. In 2003, 3.4 million voters signed a petition stating their dissatisfaction with the Chávez administration. But rioting erupted after the National Electoral Council declared that nearly half of those signatures were invalid or fake and had to be checked. Chávez's opponents said he was trying to prevent the referendum from happening. Eventually, the recall vote was set for August 15, 2004. A

Hugo Chávez Frías remains a very controversial figure in Venezuelan politics.

> Visit www.vgsbooks.com to find links to resources on Venezuela's history and government, including their constitution, voting practices, and the controversy surrounding Chávez's presidency.

record number of Venezuelans turned out to vote. Chávez won the majority of the votes and will remain in power through 2006.

Government

The Bolivarian Republic of Venezuela is a federal republic with five branches of government—the executive, the legislative, the judicial, the citizen, and the electoral. The president and the legislature are directly elected by the people in national elections. Voting is open to all Venezuelans eighteen years of age or older, but voter turnout is often less than 50 percent.

The 1999 constitution gives the executive branch more power than the other branches of Venezuela's government. The president is elected to a six-year term of office as the chief of state and head of government. He or she can be reelected to a second term. The president selects a vice president and appoints a twenty-four-member Council of Ministers.

Venezuela has a unicameral (one-house) elected legislature, called the National Assembly, which consists of 165 members. The 1999 constitution guarantees a representative number of those seats to members of indigenous groups. The Supreme Tribunal of Justice, whose twenty members are appointed to twelve-year terms by the National Assembly, exercises judicial power. The National Assembly also appoints members of the Citizens Branch and the Electoral Branch. The Citizens Branch includes an ombudsman who investigates complaints of human rights violations and other abuses suspected of public officials. The National Electoral Council organizes all elections.

Administratively, Venezuela is subdivided into twenty-three states, the federal district of Caracas, and a federal dependency consisting of seventy-two nearby islands. Voters in each state elect a governor and a state legislature.

Venezuela has had twenty-seven constitutions since 1811. Under the Constitution of 1961, the president was elected to a five-year term of office and could not immediately have a second term. The president was only eligible for reelection after an interval of ten years (two terms). This is why many former presidents reappeared later in Venezuela's history.

THE PEOPLE

From 1970 to 1985, Venezuela's population increased at an annual rate of 2.7 percent—one of the highest growth rates in South America. An economic slump and political turmoil dissuaded families from adding more members. As a result, the population growth slowed to 1.9 percent. Venezuela's population was estimated at 25.7 million in 2003. At its current pace of expansion, it should reach 41.7 million by 2050.

Although its birthrate is slowing down, Venezuela, like most Latin American countries, has a sizable young population. About 34 percent of Venezuelans are younger than 15 years of age. (In 1965 that percentage was 46 percent.) Venezuela's high fertility rate—2.8 children for each woman of childbearing age (15 to 49)—has led to vigorous family-planning education. Only a small percentage of the female population, however, uses any form of birth control, and abortion is illegal. Divorce is common in Venezuela, and multiple generations of families, with children from previous relations, often live together under one roof.

◉ Ethnic Mixture

About 67 percent of Venezuela's population is classified as mestizo, or a combination of Indian, Spanish, and African bloodlines. A high percentage of mestizos live in the rural areas. About 21 percent of Venezuelans are of European (primarily Spanish) ancestry and are heavily concentrated in the cities. Traditionally, this group has controlled Venezuela's political, social, and economic life. Blacks—whose African ancestors were brought to Venezuela as slaves—represent 10 percent of the population and live mostly in coastal areas, including the Maracaibo Lowlands.

Only 2 percent of the population are classified as purely indigenous, even though nearly thirty different indigenous groups exist. Soon after the Spanish conquest, the largest indigenous groups were worked to extinction. Small numbers fled to the inaccessible jungle, where some tribes already lived. Surviving indigenous peoples in Venezuela live mainly in remote highland areas of the country and in the rain forests of Amazonas State.

A **Warao Indian family** prepares *palmito* (hearts of palm) for their meal. For links that offer more information about Venezuela's indigenous populations, visit www.vgsbooks.com.

The Warao and the Wayúu, or the Guajíra, are the largest native groups still left in Venezuela. The Warao live in the Orinoco Delta (Delta Amacuro State) of northeast Venezuela. The Wayúu live mainly in the western section of the Lake Maracaibo Basin and continue to be nomadic herders. In 2004 Colombian groups slaughtered dozens of Wayúu Indians living in the Guajíra Peninsula, a coveted region in the country's illegal drug trafficking industry. Over three hundred Wayúu have since sought refuge on the Venezuelan side of the border. The most high-profile native group, however, is the Yanomami, who still maintain the seminomadic lifestyles of their ancestors. The Yanomami survive on the rich resources of the Amazon River and surrounding rain forest near the border of Venezuela and Brazil. When gold was discovered in the region in the 1980s, gold miners took over and destroyed many of the forest's resources and accidentally brought deadly diseases into Yanomami communities.

Some indigenous groups have contact with outsiders—such as miners, scientists, and missionaries—who enter their homelands. Most indigenous people strive to maintain their customs and traditional dress, but it's not uncommon to see some individuals sporting T-shirts and shorts. Other groups reject any outside influences. The Motilón, for example, live along the border of Venezuela and Colombia and resist all contact with strangers—even to the point of shooting arrows to keep people away.

¿HABLA ESPAÑOL?

The primary language of most Venezuelans is Spanish. Many indigenous groups have their own languages as well. English is taught in schools but is mostly spoken in larger cities by foreigners or in business transactions.

Rich and Poor

The contrasts between the rich and the poor of Venezuela are clearly visible in Caracas. Wealthy families in the capital live in modern, high-rise apartment buildings staffed by uniformed domestic servants, while the poor live in hillside ranchos. Wealthy Venezuelans shop at well-stocked supermarkets and department stores. The rich of Caracas enjoy sports cars, diverse entertainment, and frequent trips abroad.

The same Caracas that supports these comfortable lifestyles is ringed by barrios, communities of an increasingly unemployed and impoverished population. The number of poor people has increased rapidly in

Some of the **shantytowns** that circle Caracas have become working-class communities with electricity and drinking water. However, most still lack such basic commodities.

IMMIGRATION

The need for laborers created two major immigration movements into Venezuela. The first wave was from 1948 to 1958. The second came during the 1970s oil industry boom. Some groups immigrated to Venezuela to take refuge from the political and economic conditions of their homelands. Most immigrants come from Colombia, Spain, Italy, and Portugal. Smaller numbers also emigrated from Lebanon, Chile, Uruguay, Argentina, and Cuba. Illegal immigration, especially from Colombia, is a big challenge. Illegal immigrants, or *indocumentados*, are often mistreated and forced to live in the poor conditions of the barrios.

recent years, partly because of the large influx of illegal immigrants from neighboring Colombia, where job opportunities are few. Despite the downturn in Venezuela's economy, the demand for unskilled labor has remained high.

Venezuela's middle class is large and fairly active compared to the middle-income groups of other South American nations. Moreover, about one million European immigrants from nations such as Spain, Italy, and Portugal have settled in Caracas since the 1950s. These immigrants have further strengthened the median-income group.

Venezuelans often claim that the divisions between groups in contemporary Venezuela have more to do with money than with ethnicity. But the poor are often the same ethnic groups that have been oppressed throughout most of Venezuela's history. Socially, the gap between the attitudes and values of the rich and the poor has widened significantly since President Hugo Chávez's time in office. His programs to redistribute the country's oil wealth has caused tension between middle-class professionals and the working class, who cling to the administration's promises of wealth and land for all Venezuelans.

Rural Life

The city limits of Caracas mark a boundary between two worlds. Beyond the capital lies a typically agricultural society, except for a handful of secondary cities that support considerable industry. Rural Venezuela is composed of quiet towns and villages. Land is in the hands of a few, and most agricultural laborers produce crops only for their own needs on rented or unclaimed land.

The pace of life is slower in Venezuela's villages. They were established long ago to serve the coffee growers of the highlands and the sugarcane and cacao plantations of the lower elevations.

Farming in Venezuela is done in much the same way it was three hundred years ago. Farmers still harvest their crops by hand and till the soil with wooden plows attached to oxen.

Geographically isolated, the people of rural Venezuela value conservative ideals and traditional lifestyles.

Health

The infant mortality rate of Venezuela is 20 deaths in every 1,000 live births—a lower ratio than many other countries in South America. The average life span of a Venezuelan born in 2003 was about 73 years of age. This is an improvement over past figures.

In 2001 only 0.5 percent of the population was reportedly infected with AIDS (acquired immunodeficiency syndrome). The actual number of people with AIDS could be much higher. Diseases caused by insects, such as malaria, have largely been controlled by insecticides. A vaccination campaign has also decreased the number of polio and tuberculosis cases. Government efforts to improve environmental conditions by filling disease-spreading ponds and by providing clean drinking water have also created better health conditions. In modern, urban areas, Venezuelans are more likely to die from heart disease, cancer, and car accidents.

Medical care is good but expensive and is concentrated mostly in the cities. Private and public facilities exist, but medical supplies are

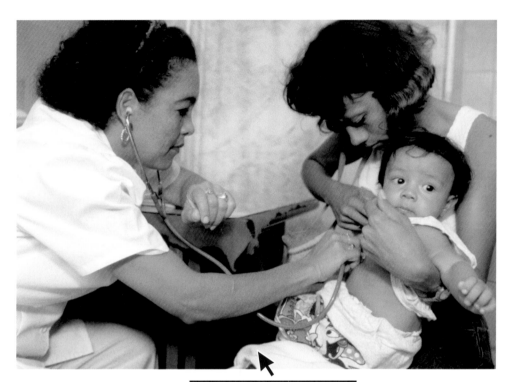

A young child receives a checkup at a medical clinic. For links that give more information about health care in Venezuela, visit www.vgsbooks.com.

limited. The Venezuelan Institute of Social Security and the Ministry of Health and Social Welfare provide most health care. Statistically, 2.4 doctors exist for every 1,000 people, and 1.5 hospital beds are available for every 1,000 Venezuelans. These figures are for populations in urban not rural areas. Nurse's aides and recent medical school graduates were the most frequently found medical personnel in the countryside. Since the end of the 1990s, however, thousands of Cuban doctors have volunteered to work in Venezuela's Cuban-style health program. These volunteers run free neighborhood clinics in rural and working-class areas. The government is also building new clinics in these areas. Indigenous people, especially in the Amazon rain forest, often use medicinal plants to treat illness among themselves.

Education

In 1992 the Venezuelan government devoted more than 23 percent of its national expenses to public education. In 1998, however, spending dropped to a mere 3.8 percent. Nevertheless, about 93 percent of all Venezuelans are literate (able read and write). Adults born before improvements in education and residents of remote rural regions are often still illiterate. To erase adult illiteracy, the government designed a massive literacy program involving more than four million students and thousands of volunteers. Special evening classes are available at all school levels.

While primary education (ages six to fifteen) and secondary education (ages fifteen to seventeen) are free, enrollment drops to less than 40 percent after the first ten years. Many blame the dropout rate on the weakened economy. Corruption and educators' dissatisfaction with educational reform have added to the system's problems. Facilities need to be updated, and teachers' wages remain low. In 2001 teacher strikes crippled the educational system, cutting in half the amount of time spent in class.

With the proceeds of oil profits, the Venezuelan government supports full scholarships annually for more than one thousand promising young students to pursue their academic careers at universities abroad. Such support, however, is conditional—the students pledge to return to Venezuela to practice their professions.

Venezuela has eighteen public universities, fifteen privately supported universities, and at least one hundred other institutions of higher learning. The centerpiece of higher education is the Central University in Caracas, which has a beautifully landscaped setting with modern buildings and the latest in educational equipment. The total enrollment at the universities is more than 600,000, which represents a 50 percent increase during the past decade. Venezuelan women outnumber men in institutions of higher learning. More women than ever are doctors, lawyers, and engineers, but they don't always hold high-level positions.

WOMAN'S RIGHTS

Women began to take an active role in Venezuelan society in the early 1900s. In the 1940s, they created the Venezuelan Women's Association. A major victory for woman's rights was granted in 1947, when Venezuelan women were given the right to vote. Although still expected to fulfill traditional roles in a household, many contemporary Venezuelan women have become more politically active. They fight for issues such as equal rights for all Venezuelans, an end to domestic abuse, and better access to health care and child care.

CULTURAL LIFE

Venezuela's vibrant culture is a unique combination of traditions from indigenous groups, Africans, European colonialists, and pop culture. While music and sports from other parts of the world, such as the United States, are increasing in popularity, Venezuelan music and telenovelas, or soap operas, have gained worldwide attention. Venezuela has also produced talented artists and writers.

Art

Indigenous groups produced some of Venezuela's earliest art around 1000 B.C. After Spanish colonization in the 1500s and before Venezuela's independence in the early 1800s, most Venezuelan art was religious in theme. Artists later focused on portraits, historical scenes, and landscapes. The Venezuelan artist Armando Reverón stands out for his treatment of color in landscapes.

Some Venezuelan artists adopted the social themes of *indigenismo*. This early twentieth-century South American cultural movement

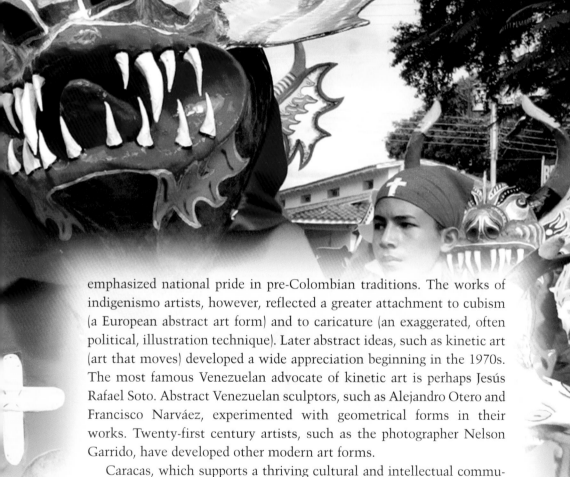

emphasized national pride in pre-Colombian traditions. The works of indigenismo artists, however, reflected a greater attachment to cubism (a European abstract art form) and to caricature (an exaggerated, often political, illustration technique). Later abstract ideas, such as kinetic art (art that moves) developed a wide appreciation beginning in the 1970s. The most famous Venezuelan advocate of kinetic art is perhaps Jesús Rafael Soto. Abstract Venezuelan sculptors, such as Alejandro Otero and Francisco Narváez, experimented with geometrical forms in their works. Twenty-first century artists, such as the photographer Nelson Garrido, have developed other modern art forms.

Caracas, which supports a thriving cultural and intellectual community, has become the place where Venezuelan artists obtain national recognition. The city expanded greatly in the twentieth century, and its public buildings reflect both the benefits of oil profits and a new architectural style. The design of Central University in Caracas displays the work of some of Venezuela's greatest artists and the talent of its most

"Estudio del balcon" (Study of the Balcony), was painted by **Cristóbal Rojas.**

influential architect, Carlos Raúl Villanueva. The greatest collection of Venezuelan paintings is found in the Museum of Fine Arts in Caracas. On exhibition are paintings by Arturo Michelena, Cristóbal Rojas, Martín Tovar y Tovar, Francisco Valdés, Antonio Herrera Toro, José María Ver León, and Tito Salas.

Literature

Venezuela's literature has its roots in the stories of its indigenous people, who passed on their traditions and culture orally. The earliest written works were done after the Spaniards established themselves in the area. They wrote mostly descriptions of the region. One of the first Venezuelan books—*Calendario manuel y guía universel de forasteros en Caracas para 1810*—contains a history of Venezuela by the noted classical scholar Andrés Bello. Bello later wrote the poem "Silva a la agricultura de la zona" ("Ode to the Agriculture of the Torrid Zone"), and in 1843 he produced the sentimental *Prayer for All.* An early printing press was set up on Margarita Island for Simón Bolívar. The press issued his proclamations and other historic documents.

In the nineteenth century, romanticism—a movement that glorified events in sentimental language—became extremely popular in much of South America. In Venezuela this style focused on the independence era. Representative of this school were the works of Juan

Vicente González, Eduardo Blanco, Abigaíl Lozano, and José Antonio Pérez Bonalde. A lesser-known movement called *criollismo* also thrived in Venezuela. In sharp contrast to romanticism, this style was noted for its realism and its focus on unsentimental Venezuelan scenes. *Peonía,* a novel by Manuel Vicente Romero Garcia, was at the forefront of this style, which later developed a critical side.

One of the best-known South American novelists at the beginning of the twentieth century was Manuel Díaz Rodríguez, with his precise poetic style. Another leading twentieth-century literary figure was the talented novelist and former president, Rómulo Gallegos, author of *La trepadora, Canaima,* and *Pobre negro.* His best-known work is *Doña Bárbara,* whose heroine struggles to impose civilization on the wilderness of the plains. Other notable writers of this time include novelist Teresa de la Parra and essayist Mariano Picón Salas.

Most writers eventually abandoned pastoral settings for more urban backgrounds. Their works depict the effects of oil profits on a once largely agricultural land. Writers such as Arturo Uslar Pietri stands out. In the 1960s, Salvador Garmendia's novels examined the increasing problems of urban life. Writers in the last half of the twentieth century experimented more with style and developed themes that reflected the social and political climate of the time.

The Media

Modern media outlets, including newspapers, television, and film, have the most influence on Venezuelans. In 1808 James Lamb and Matthew Gallagher printed the first newspaper in Venezuela, the *Gazeta de Caracas* (Caracas Gazette). This paper, along with the others that followed, were controlled by the interests of the prevailing government. They experienced periods of censorship and closure at the hands of Venezuela's dictators. The dictatorships of Juan Vicente Gómez in the early 1900s and Marcos Pérez Jiménez in the 1950s were especially repressive to free speech. The top newspapers in the twenty-first century are *El Universal* and *El Nacional,* both out of Caracas. In other cities, newspaper such as *Ultimas Noticias, Panorama,* and *El Tiempo* also provide Venezuelans with daily news.

During the Chávez presidency, radio and television news organizations have entered politics. The government maintains an antagonistic relationship with the privately run media, which say that the administration has threatened and bullied them. Chávez supporters claim that the media outlets have created a gross distortion of his presidency.

Meanwhile, the more than one hundred FM radio stations play a wide variety of music. AM stations, which are twice as abundant, have become forums for discussion. Privately run radio stations in

AND THE WINNER IS . . .

Venezuelan beauty queens are groomed from a young age. Pageants are commonplace, and aspiring models can even attend special schools to help them hone their pageant skills. Since the mid-1900s, Venezuela has produced four Miss Universe winners, along with numerous Miss World and Miss International titles. Pageant winners have bright futures. For Irene Sáez, Miss Universe 1981 *(below)*, the title was the springboard for an esteemed political career. Sáez later became the mayor of a city near Caracas and the governor of Nueva Esparta State. She even ran for the presidency in 1998.

the barrios broadcast pro-Chávez programs.

Television appeals widely to Venezuelans, who have greater access to television than any other Latin American country. Major television organizations and networks include the government-run Venezolana de Televisión and the privately owned and operated Venevisión, Radio Caracas Televisión, NCTV, Televén, and Globovisión. Cable and satellite also offer a wide range of programming.

Foreign programs take up a large share of programming, but for most Venezuelans, telenovelas dominate the viewing hours. Over half of Venezuelans admit to watching them regularly. Occasionally, a telenovela, such as *Por estas calles* (Along These Streets), makes references to the political and social situation of the country. But most programs rely on romance or sensationalized drama to attract viewers.

Programs such as *Cristal, Kassandra, La dama de Rosa,* and *Aunque me cueste la vida* (Though It May Cost Me My Life) have kept viewers in Venezuela and abroad glued to their sets every day. The celebrity of a soap star, much like that of a former Venezuelan beauty queen, grants all sorts of opportunities. Former soap stars have become successful musicians and even politicians. *Farándula* (a form of tabloid gossip) about soap stars such as Eileen Abad, Rosalinda Serfaty, and Miguel de León have made them household names.

The film industry in Venezuela has yet to reach the overwhelming popularity of its television industry. Filmmakers have been forced to seek government support to finance their films and to get them played in cinemas. (Most cinemas show foreign films, such as Hollywood blockbusters.) Nevertheless, since the 1950s, many Venezuelan filmmakers have produced internationally acclaimed films that focus on social and political issues. Some of the more recognizable filmmakers from Venezuela include Margot Benacerraf, Román Chalbaud, Clemente de la Cerda, Diego Rísquez, Fina Torres, Carlos Azpúrua, and Luis Alberto Lamata.

◉ Music and Dance

Dance and music, especially Venezuela's distinctive folk music and popular songs, surround all major events. Much of the country's folk music comes from the *llaneros* (people of the plains), who sing songs about the wide, open spaces of Venezuela. Venezuelan folk dancing and music—including the *joropo* (the national dance), the *carite,* and the *gaita zuliana*—have strong ties to homemade instruments, which are fashioned from a wide variety of materials. The most popular Venezuelan musical instruments are the guitar, the harp, and a small, four-stringed guitar called a *cuatro.* Harp player Juan Vicente Torreabla and balladeer Simón Díaz are among the musicians who have brought the music of the plains into the mainstream.

Music with strong drumbeats, such as the calypso, is a reflection

THE REVOLUTION WILL NOT BE TELEVISED

One of the most significant films to come out of Venezuela in the early 2000s is a documentary by two Irish directors, Donncha Ó Briain and Kim Bartley. Released in 2003, *The Revolution Will Not Be Televised*, or *Chavez: Inside the Coup*, captures the 2002 coup against the government of Hugo Chávez. The filmmakers experienced the coup firsthand from inside the presidential palace. The controversial documentary takes a pro-Chávez stance. The private news media tends to broadcast anti-Chávez material.

Venezuelans dance the **joropo,** the national dance, outside the Miraflores presidential palace.

of African culture. Salsa music and dance also enjoy great popularity in Venezuela, and Oscar D'Leon emerged as one of the most recognizable salsa singers in the world. Classical music lovers can enjoy the sounds of any of Venezuela's dozens of professional symphony orchestras.

Religion and Festivals

Roman Catholicism, which was brought by Spanish and European missionaries, is the official religion of the country. Nearly 96 percent of the population call themselves Catholic. Although freedom of religion has existed in Venezuela since 1834, only 2 percent of Venezuelans are Protestant. About 2 percent follow other religions, such as Islam, Judaism, and the cult of María Lionza. The latter combines spirit worship, legends from indigenous groups, and African beliefs with Catholicism. Although missionaries continue to work in areas inhabited by indigenous groups, most indigenous people still maintain their own religious practices.

The Roman Catholic Church has enjoyed periods of considerable political and social influence. The church has experienced periods of tension between governing groups, which feared the church's powerful influence over Venezuelans. The church has since been an active participant in political affairs, and leaders speak out frequently in support of social reform. The Venezuelan government is active in the selection of church officials.

Most Venezuelans do not regularly attend church services, but they turn to the church in times of crisis or to perform rites such as baptisms, marriages, and funerals. Venezuelans' informal observance of Catholic rites dates back to the presidencies of Antonio Guzmán Blanco and his push for secularization (to transfer power of the church to civilians) in the 1870s. Families worshiped at their leisure and in the privacy of their own home. When freedom of religion was restored, most Venezuelans continued their home worship. Catholic rites are still the focus of many holiday festivities.

Numerous festivals are held throughout the year in Venezuela. The biggest holidays are Christmas in December and Carnival, which is celebrated prior to the beginning of Lent (the period of fasting and penance before Easter). During Carnival, singing and dancing are widespread in the streets of most cities and towns, and parades of colorful

Beatriz Viet-Tane, a mystic who created the cult of María Lionza, performs rites with her followers in the 1960s. The goddess María Lionza is a symbol of love, fertility, and nature. Originally named Lara, the goddess is said to have been a princess who was kidnapped by a giant anaconda snake. Her capture angered the mountain gods, who made the snake swell until it burst. Lara was then named queen of rivers, waterfalls, and lakes.

SAINT BOLÍVAR

Images of saints are ever present in Venezuelan homes, wallets, shops, and cars. Venezuelans give offerings and pray to countless saints (*above*) for help with their health, finances, love life, and even politics. Some of these figures, such as the Virgin Mary, Madre María de San José, and José Gregario Hernández are acceptable to the Catholic Church. Cultlike worship is frowned upon, however. Mostly because it combines spiritual and magical elements. Members of the cult of María Lionza worship a blend of African, indigenous, and Catholic figures. Many Venezuelans have even given Simón Bolívar saintlike status in their lives, as he is supposed to bring financial and political advice.

floats crowd the main square. Confetti, candy, and many popular amusements further contribute to the festival atmosphere.

Each celebration has its own costumes and customs. In Zulia State, the saint San Benito de Palermo is celebrated with dancing and music (drumming in particular) of African roots. Grotesque masks and red clothes are a feature of the Dancing Devils—an Indian-inspired entertainment performed in San Francisco de Yare on the Catholic feast of Corpus Christi.

◉ Food

Venezuelan cuisine, known as *cocino criollo*, varies from region to region. Venezuela's tropical climate is ideal for growing many kinds of fruits. Venezuelans can find pineapples, papayas, passion fruit, plantains, and many other fruits sold on the street or in large markets. On the coasts and the islands, fish and seafood are abundant and found in most dishes.

AREPAS

Arepas are a type of round, flat corn bread made from corn flour and water. Arepas can be filled with cheese, meats, fruits, or other ingredients.

2 cups corn flour (precooked yellow or white mesa flour)

1 teaspoon salt

2 cups cool water

vegetable oil

½ cup grated white cheese

1. In a large mixing bowl, whisk together the flour and salt. Stir in enough water (approximately 2 cups) to make a firm, slightly moist dough.
2. Cover the dough with a clean dish cloth, and let it sit for 5 minutes.
3. Divide the dough into 10 pieces, and form each piece into a ball. Flatten the ball slightly.
4. Preheat the oven to 350°F.
5. Oil a griddle very lightly, and warm it over medium heat.
6. Cook the arepas on the griddle for about 5 minutes on each side, until a golden brown crust forms.
7. Transfer the arepas to a baking sheet and bake 15 to 25 minutes, turning them several times as they bake. Tap them when you think they're done. They should sound hollow. Remove from the oven.
8. Split open the arepas, and remove some of the inside dough. Fill with cheese and serve immediately.

Serves 10

Llaneros eat the beef from the cattle raised in the Llanos. Many indigenous groups choose from the vast array of plants, animals, and even insects found in the rain forest.

Arepas are a staple of Venezuelan cuisine. They are round, flat pieces of bread made from corn flour. They are served at any time of the day and sold at street corner stands called *areperas* and in restaurants. Arepas are eaten plain or filled with meat, cheese, eggs, vegetables, or any other tasty ingredient.

Other favorite treats include *pabelló criollo* and *hallacas*. Pabelló criollo—made with beef, rice, black beans, cheese, and fried plantains—is considered the national dish of Venezuela. Steamed hallacas, made with meat, vegetables, and cornmeal dough and wrapped in

Venezuelans enjoy a wide **variety of foods,** from tropical fruits and fresh fish to deep-fried ants and cheeses made from water buffalo milk.

banana leaves, are a staple of Christmas. Popular drinks include beer, rum, espresso coffee, and fruit drinks.

Venezuelans sometimes indulge in Western-style fast food sold at restaurants such as McDonald's, KFC, and Pizza Hut. Higher-end foreign restaurants serve Spanish, Italian, Middle Eastern, and Chinese food.

Sports and Recreation

Baseball and basketball dominate Venezuela's recreational activities. Most towns and all cities have their own stadiums, where professional and amateur teams play. Venezuelans also have the luxury of watching their favorite sports year-round. Loyal Venezuelan baseball fans can follow major league games in the United States during the regular baseball season and Venezuela's own teams during its winter league. Famous Venezuelan baseball players in *las grandes ligas* (the big leagues) include Alfonso "Chico" Carrasquel, Adrés "El Gato" (The Cat) Galarraga, Omar Vizquel, and Luís Sojo. The basketball season runs in a similar way—with the Venezuelan basketball season running during the off-season for the U.S. NBA. Soccer draws a much smaller audience than it does in other Latin American nations, but soccer fervor occurs every four years when the FIFA World Cup takes place.

To learn more about Venezuelan cultural life, visit www.vgsbooks.com. You'll find links to information on Venezuela's art, food and recipes, holidays and festivals, baseball, and more.

Bullfighting draws large crowds and top-ranking international matadors to the rings. Bullfighting events are usually organized in connection with a fair or festival. In Caracas, Maracaibo, and Valencia, horse races draw large crowds of wealthy and well-dressed spectators. People watch the track with excitement and place their bets on their favorite horses to win.

Water sports are very popular with Venezuelans, who flock to the seaside for holidays. Swimming, diving, waterskiing, windsurfing, and game fishing are enjoyed all year. Margarita Island boasts one of the world's greatest windsurfing locations at Playa El Yaque. First-rate game fishing draws international participants. Tuna, marlin, trout, and dorado are prized catches.

The Andean mountains in northwestern Venezuela provide challenges for sports enthusiasts. Mountain climbers find many peaks and rocky crags to scale. Skiers take advantage of frequent snowfalls that cover Pico Bolívar nearly every day between May and October.

Baseball became Venezuela's favorite spectator sport in large part because of the oil industry. Executives from U.S. oil companies brought the sport with them in the early 1900s.

THE ECONOMY

With per capita earnings (the average amount of money a person earns in a year) of more than $5,590, Venezuela statistically ranks among the most economically advanced countries of Latin America. The figure, however, masks deep inequalities in the division of wealth, which is heavily concentrated in the hands of a small minority. At the end of 2003, nearly 18 percent of Venezuela's workforce was unemployed, and about 80 percent of Venezuelans lived in poverty. Political unrest, especially since the coup of 2002 and the oil strikes of 2003, has created an economic uncertainty that has discouraged investments in new industries.

▶ Venezuela's Oil Industry

Oil became the focus of the economy soon after Venezuela's first commercial oil drilling in 1917. By 1926 petroleum had replaced coffee as Venezuela's principal export, but abuse of power and position to gain oil profits became widespread. Government corruption did not stop even in 1976, when Venezuela nationalized all of its oil fields.

The Venezuelan economy experienced a serious battering in the 1980s and early 1990s because of a decline in earnings from its oil exports. When world oil prices crashed in the early 1980s, Venezuela's economy plummeted. The bolívar (the official currency) fell in value, and Venezuelans saw their incomes decrease. Gone was the big spending of the 1970s, with exorbitant shopping excursions to foreign countries such as the United States. Inflation was rampant. A recession, or period of reduced economic activity, in the late 1980s only worsened conditions, and President Carlos Andrés Pérez's attempts to develop other industries ultimately failed. The 1990s brought a 1,000 percent increase in gas prices, and the oil industry had to be reopened to foreign investors. The shortfall in oil revenues increased spiraling foreign debts. Eventually, rising oil prices and increased production in the mid-1990s led to four straight years of growth in export revenues. Between 1995 and 1997, Venezuela pushed oil production from 2.3 to 3 million barrels per day.

NATIONALIZATION

During the early 1970s, foreign oil companies paid Venezuela $1 billion a year to remove oil, mostly from the Maracaibo area. This region accounted for over 70 percent of the crude oil production. Twenty-one companies—most of them U.S. owned—were engaged in the production of crude oil.

In 1975 Venezuela decided to nationalize the oil industry. By 1976 Venezuelan Petroleum (PETROVEN), the federally owned oil monopoly, had assumed control of the nation's oil industry.

The nationalization process was achieved on friendly terms. Many of the foreign companies contracted with PETROVEN to provide it with technical assistance and marketing outlets. The company, renamed Petróleos de Venezuela, S.A. (PDVSA), continues to rely on foreign firms for technical help.

In January 2002, a new hydrocarbons law went into effect. It opened up the extra-heavy crude petroleum industry to partnerships with private investors but at a much higher cost. Opponents say this will discourage foreign investment.

When Hugo Chávez was elected president in 1998, he promised to bring some of the oil wealth back to the poorer classes. However, while inflation and poverty went down, crime shot up. Venezuela experienced a recession.

Venezuela's government-owned oil company, Petróleos de Venezuela, S.A. (PDVSA), staged a strike in 2002 to oppose Chávez's appointments to high-level PDVSA positions. The strike resulted in a brief coup and, along with another strike that year, devastated the petroleum industry. Despite the country's return to its high prestrike production levels, Venezuela has not yet fully recovered from the strikes. Chávez fired over fifteen thousand PDVSA employees, and it will take a long time to replace their knowledge and expertise. Chávez has since tried to woo foreign investors back to Venezuela.

In 2004 Venezuela was one of the top ten oil producers and exporters in the world. Official estimates of Venezuela's oil production are from 2.1 to 2.8 million barrels a day, with a goal of over 5 million barrels by 2008. Venezuela's oil reserves are estimated to be close to 80 billion barrels, and an additional 100 to 270 billion barrels of extra-heavy crude oil have been found in the Orinoco Heavy Oil Belt.

◉ Other Industries

At the beginning of the twenty-first century, all industries (including the petroleum industry) accounted for about 23 percent of the country's total employment and 35 percent of the gross domestic product (GDP—the value of goods and services produced by Venezuela in a year). Included in these totals are mining, manufacturing, and power. Petroleum and petroleum by-products account for most mining and processing receipts but employ a small percentage of workers.

Venezuela also has huge natural gas reserves, some of the largest in the world. Bauxite—from which aluminum is made—is exploited in the Guiana Highlands. Important gold mines are located southeast of Bolívar State. New deposits were discovered in the early 1960s near El Callao in the Guiana Highlands. Diamonds are found in Venezuela's Amazonas State, and high-grade phosphate rock has been found in Falcón State. Sulfur deposits are located in the state of Sucre, and nickel mines are sited near Las Tejerías. Venezuela is also known to have deposits of manganese, copper, and asbestos. Coal is mined in the states of Táchira, Aragua, and Anzoátegui and large coal reserves exist in the state of Zulia.

Perhaps most important for continuous stability in Venezuela's economy is the development of manufacturing industries. Before the 1960s, most Venezuelan oil was refined abroad, and natural gas was burned off or wasted. Domestic oil refineries have been established since then. Natural gas is distributed by pipeline for use as fuel, as raw material for the petrochemical industry, and as part of the manufacturing of liquid gas. The Maracaibo area operates most of the nation's refineries.

Morón, situated about 100 miles (160 km) west of La Guaira, is the center of Venezuela's petrochemical industry. Products include fertilizers, insecticides, explosives, soda (a salt used for making soap products, glass, and paper), and other chemicals.

The processing of foods, the rebuilding of heavy machinery, and the production of paper, electrical equipment, and pharmaceuticals are

OPEC

In 1960 Venezuela became a founding member of the Organization of Petroleum Exporting Countries (OPEC). This multinational organization sets prices and establishes production quotas (limits) for member countries—Venezuela, Iran, Iraq, Kuwait, Qatar, Saudi Arabia, United Arab Emirates, Algeria, Libya, Nigeria, and Indonesia. Without such controls, member countries could produce any amount of oil they want, which would decrease the demand for oil and thus lower oil prices. In reality, many OPEC members produce more than the quota to take advantage of high prices. Since helping to establish the organization in 1960, Venezuela has been fairly cooperative (with lapses after the 2002 strike) in keeping oil production below OPEC quotas.

concentrated in the Maracaibo area. Venezuela fills about 90 percent of its domestic demand for processed beverages, tobacco, clothing, and textiles. Paper and cardboard production amount to about 612,000 tons (555,200 metric tons) annually, and factories assemble about 68,000 automotive vehicles each year.

Until the 1960s, manufacturing was largely concentrated in Caracas. Since then, the government has promoted the distribution of heavy industry to other parts of the country. Ciudad Guayana, at the junction of the Caroní and the Orinoco rivers, has been developed as an industrial complex to process iron ore mined in the Guiana Highlands. After the iron ore has been dug out of the earth, it is transported to plants for further refinement into steel or crude iron. Most of the iron ore is mined for export. A government-owned steel plant turns out structural steel, reinforcing rods, rails, steel sheets and tubes, and seamless steel pipes for the petroleum industry. Cement-processing plants are also in operation, and an oil refinery and a petrochemical complex have been installed at Ciudad Guayana.

Several electric furnaces, using power generated by the hydroelectric plant at the Gurí Dam on the Caroní River, manufacture iron into products needed by industry. The Gurí Dam is 500 feet (152 m) high and supplies water to twenty-four generators. In addition to its

The Gurí Dam was built in 1963. Together with Macagua II, the dam provides Venezuela with 70 percent of its electrical needs. The dam's reservoir is South America's fourth largest lake and is a popular place for sportfishing.

use in steel manufacturing, electric power helps fuel the area's aluminum complexes, which receive bauxite from mines in the Guiana Highlands. More than 630,000 tons (570,000 metric tons) per year of aluminum were manufactured in the late 1990s.

Venezuela's greatest economic progress since the 1960s has been in developing a framework of highways, pipelines, power lines, and hydroelectric plants to serve the expanding needs of the nation's mineral producers. As proven reserves of oil, gas, iron ore, and bauxite have expanded, the government has encouraged the installation of the equipment needed to process these materials.

Agriculture, Livestock, and Fishing

Profits from agriculture contribute less than 5 percent to Venezuela's total national income, and agricultural activities provide work for only about 10 percent of the labor force. Over 50 percent of all farmers are engaged in subsistence production, meaning they grow crops only for their own needs. This is especially true in the Andes, where few stretches of level land exist. Permanent crops, such as citrus groves, fill 19 percent of all farmland, while the remainder either is left unused or is under temporary cultivation. Betancourt's administration enacted an agrarian reform law in 1960 that aimed to broaden and modernize Venezuela's agricultural production. Recent government programs have aimed to increase Venezuela's production of food, including tropical fruits.

Despite decades of agrarian reform in Venezuela, growth rates in agricultural output barely keep pace with population expansion, and the rural population has continued to decline. Consequently, imported food makes up about two-thirds of the country's total consumption. Farmworkers are in demand, and illegal immigrants continue to enter the agricultural sector from Colombia and other countries.

Venezuela's agricultural and pastureland zones contribute in different ways to food production. Principal crops in the agricultural zone are coffee, cacao, sugarcane, maize (corn), rice, wheat, tobacco, cotton, beans, and sisal (rope fiber).

The pastureland areas, mostly in the Llanos, afford grazing for 16 million cattle and 500,000 horses. In 2002 the livestock count for the nation showed 5.7 million pigs, 4 million goats, 820,000 sheep, and 115 million poultry. Over three-fourths of the land used in farming is pastureland.

The waters of Venezuela are rich in fish resources, and production of canned and fresh fish doubled in the 1990s. Most fishing activities are clustered around large port cities, such as Maracaibo, and on the

Paraguaná Peninsula. Porlamar on Margarita Island is noted for its pearl fisheries, but sardines and tuna are the most important national fish catches.

Services

The service industry of Venezuela receives little attention in the world news compared to the petroleum industry. Yet services provide over 60 percent of Venezuela's GDP and employ 67 percent of the workforce. Included in these totals are workers in education, health care, retail, transportation, trade, and tourism.

Tourism receipts have plummeted since 1998, as the country's political and economic climate continues to drive away tourists and investors. Incidents of violence and robbery against foreigners, especially in large cities like Caracas, have also taken a toll on tourism. In 2000 most tourists originated from Germany, the United States, the Netherlands, Canada, the United Kingdom, and Venezuela's neighboring countries. Foreigners visit Venezuela primarily for its fantastic weather, beautiful beaches, and spectacular wildlife. The

Once flocked to because of its rich pearl beds, **Margarita Island** continues to draw tourists because of its miles and miles of beautiful beaches.

main destination for tourists is Margarita Island, and only 20 percent of tourists ever reach the mainland.

◎ Foreign Trade

Venezuela continues to maintain a favorable balance of trade by exporting more than it imports in terms of monetary value. Petroleum remains its principal export, and the major destinations for this commodity are the United States, the Netherlands Antilles (because of its nearby oil-processing facilities off the coast of Falcón), Canada, Colombia, and Brazil.

Venezuela's principal imports are electrical and automotive machinery, manufactured goods, chemical products, and grains. One third of its imports come from the United States. Other suppliers are Colombia, Brazil, Mexico, Japan, Germany, and Italy.

◎ Transportation

In the mid-twentieth century, Venezuela developed an excellent highway network, especially in the northern and western parts of the country, where three well-paved highways exist. A section of the Pan-American Highway runs southwest from Caracas to Cúcuta, Colombia. Another highway runs along the Andean foothills from Valencia to San Cristóbal. The highway in the Llanos extends eastward along the coast from Caracas and southeastward to Ciudad Bolívar. Several branch roads supplement these main thoroughfares. Taxis, minibuses (for carpooling), and buses are available in most cities, and Caracas has a subway system. Valencia is building a light rail system.

Until 1999 there was only one 100-mile (161 km) commercial rail line in service, which linked Barquisimeto with Puerto Cabello. Work has

Most Venezuelans go home for a two-hour lunch. This creates four rush hours per day. As a result, citizens of Caracas spend much of their time sitting in large **traffic jams.**

begun on a line to connect Caracas to this line. Lines are also being built to connect Acarigua to Turén in the Andes and Morón to Riecito east of Puerto Cabello.

Coastal shipping routes and inland waterways move heavy goods. Most of the nation's foreign commerce is carried by sea. The principal ports are at Puerto Cabello, La Guaira, Maracaibo, and Puerto Ordaz. The Orinoco River and Lake Maracaibo are heavily traveled inland waterways. A frequently dredged channel keeps Lake Maracaibo open to seagoing vessels.

Two airline companies handle the majority of Venezuela's flying. Aéropostal, owned by Alas de Venezuela, and Aerovías Venezolanas, S.A. (AVENSA), serve many of Venezuela's domestic and international airports. Maiquetía (Simón Bolívar) International Airport near Caracas handles most international flights.

The Future

For the near future, oil will continue to dominate the Venezuelan economy. To assure that the country does not run out of oil, the government has been studying ways to develop hard-to-reach reserves in the Orinoco Basin. Researchers have discovered methods to pump and store the reserves, resulting in increased production. The opening of industries to foreign investors and technology will allow the country to access more of its natural resources faster.

Meanwhile, the country's government and private sector are working to develop a more varied industrial base by using oil-derived income to exploit other minerals such as iron ore. The government

Visit www.vgsbooks.com for links to discover more about Venezuela's economy. Convert U.S. dollars into the Venezuelan bolívar, learn about the oil industry, and more.

also plans to build processing plants to convert more of Venezuela's crops and minerals into finished products.

The industry with the biggest potential for growth is telecommunications (telephones and the Internet). Investors have expressed their interest in the field, especially with the privatization of the country's telecommunications company. The Venezuelan government predicts that the industry might even surpass agriculture in terms of its share of the GDP.

The unequal distribution of wealth and the memory of recent economic collapse continue to concern much of the population, but 2004 brought some relief from the recession. Unemployment went down, and the GDP went up—mostly due to record-high world oil prices. Increased sales of construction materials and automobiles also contributed to the economy's slight upturn. Only when Venezuela breaks its almost-total dependence on the oil industry, however, will the country's economic growth stabilize. Venezuelans are optimistic that their history of democracy will allow them to meet this challenge and that they will continue to utilize their wealth of resources to bring well-being to all sectors of society.

Venezuelans worry about drug trafficking. The country's long, largely unprotected border with Colombia continues to be a relatively convenient route to the cocaine markets of North America and Europe. The maze of the Orinoco River's tributaries at the delta makes catching smugglers next to impossible. Venezuelans suspect that drug gangs have bribed government officials into allowing the illegal shipments into Venezuela.

14,000 B.C.	Indigenous groups settle in the Lake Maracaibo Basin, the Andes, and the Llanos.
1000S B.C.	Indigenous people create early Venezuelan works of pottery.
A.D. 1498	Christopher Columbus lands on the northeastern mainland of Venezuela.
1499	Alonso de Ojeda travels to the region and gives the Guajira Peninsula the name Venezuela. Pearl beds are found in Cubagua Island near Venezuela's northeastern coast.
CA. 1500	Nueva Cádiz settlement is established on Cubagua Island.
1521	Spain establishes the first mainland settlement in South America in Cumaná, Venezuela.
1528	Germans exploit Venezuela's indigenous people and natural resources in their search for gold.
1550	Audiencia of Santa Fe de Bogotá is established with the land of present-day Venezuela and Colombia.
1567	Caracas is founded.
LATE 1500S	Capuchins, Jesuits, Franciscans, and Dominicans (Roman Catholic religious orders) begin to establish religious settlements to convert indigenous groups.
1580	Smallpox wipes out large populations of indigenous people.
1585	Sir Francis Drake raids Caracas.
CA. 1620	Cacao becomes a major cash crop. African slaves are brought in to work the plantations.
1669	Henry Morgan attacks and loots Maracaibo.
1749	Venezuelans begin protesting against Spanish colonial rule.
1777	A captaincy general is set up to govern the provinces of Venezuela.
1806	Francisco de Miranda leads a revolutionary expedition.
1808	Venezuela's first newspaper, the *Gazeta de Caracas* (Caracas Gazette), is published.
1811	Venezuelans declare independence from Spain and adopt a constitution.
1812	An earthquake devastates Caracas and kills ten thousand people.
1819	Simón Bolívar becomes president of newly established Gran Colombia.

1830 Venezuela breaks away from Gran Colombia, and José Antonio Páez becomes president of Venezuela.

1834 Congress grants freedom of religion.

1854 Slavery is abolished.

1870 Antonio Guzmán Blanco begins rule over Venezuela.

1878 Petroleum reserves are explored.

1902 Great Britain, Italy, and Germany blockade Venezuela's ports for non-payment of loans.

1908 Juan Vicente Gómez becomes president, beginning a long period of social repression.

1917 The first commercial oil drilling is done near Lake Maracaibo.

1922 Large petroleum deposits are found, and Venezuela's oil industry takes off.

1947 The Democratic Action Party wins power in democratic elections. Women gain the right to vote.

1959 Rómulo Betancourt becomes president.

1960 Venezuela helps found the Organization of Petroleum Exporting Countries (OPEC).

1961 Venezuelans approve a new constitution, which makes voting universal and obligatory.

1973 Venezuela experiences the beginning of an oil boom.

1976 Nationalization of Venezuela's oil industry occurs.

1983 The stock market crashes, and the oil boom of the 1970s ends.

1992 Two attempted coups are made against President Carlos Andrés Pérez.

1994 Venezuela has an economic crisis when the banking system collapses.

1999 Hugo Chávez begins his presidency. A new constitution is approved. Venezuela is renamed the Bolivarian Republic of Venezuela.

2000 Chávez is reelected to a six-year term.

2002 A coup briefly removes Chávez from power. Employees of the national oil company, Petróleos de Venezuela, strike in opposition to the Chávez administration.

2003 Chávez opponents collect signatures for a referendum, which could remove Chávez from office.

2004 Protests and strikes continue to plague the nation.

COUNTRY NAME Bolivarian Republic of Venezuela

AREA 352,144 square miles (912,050 sq. km)

MAIN LANDFORMS Andes Mountains, coastal lowlands, Llanos, Guiana Highlands

HIGHEST POINT Pico Bolívar, 16,427 feet (5,007 m) above sea level

LOWEST POINT Sea level

MAJOR RIVERS Orinoco River, Caroní River, Portuguesa River, Apure River, Arauca River, Meta River, Caura River

ANIMALS jaguars, pumas, monkeys, bears, peccaries, deer, capybaras, opossums, wild dogs, agoutis, skunks, tapir, manatees, caimans, alligators, boa constrictors, anacondas, cranes, herons, storks, guácharos, ibis, shrimps, electric eels, piranhas, sponges, anemones, coral, angelfish, barracuda

CAPITAL CITY Caracas

OTHER MAJOR CITIES Maracaibo, Valencia, Barquisimeto, Ciudad Guayana, Ciudad Bolívar

OFFICIAL LANGUAGE Spanish

MONETARY UNIT Bolívar (B). B 1 = 100 céntimos

VENEZUELAN CURRENCY

The bolívar—named to honor the revolutionary leader Simón Bolívar—is the official unit of currency in Venezuela. Notes are printed in denominations of bolívares (Bs) 5, 10, 20, 50, 100, 500, 1,000, 2,000, 5,000, 10,000, and 20,000. Coins for Bs 10, 20, 50, 100, and 500 are also available.

Currency *Fast Facts*

The Venezuelan flag dates from 1806, when Francisco de Miranda raised it as a symbol of the independence movement. The flag later represented the 1811 Confederation of Venezuela but went through many designs before the current one was adopted in 1930 and made official in 1954. The seven white stars on the middle stripe commemorate the seven original provinces of the confederation. The flag's three colored stripes symbolize the wealth (yellow) of the country, the ocean (blue) that separates Venezuela from Spain, and the blood (red) of those who fought in the revolution. The symbol in the left corner of the yellow stripe is Venezuela's coat of arms.

On May 25, 1881, the government of Venezuela adopted "Gloria al bravo pueblo" (Glory to the Brave People) as the country's national anthem. Juan José Landaeta wrote the music. The lyrics, written by Vicente Salias, exalt Venezuela's struggle for independence from Spain. Both men were executed in 1814 for their participation in the independence movement. An English translation of the chorus and the first verse of the national anthem are below.

Glory to the brave nation
Which shook off the yoke,
Respecting law, virtue and honor.

"Off with the chains! Off with the chains!"
Cried the Lord, cried the Lord,
And the poor man in his hovel
Implored freedom.
At this holy name, there trembled
The vile selfishness that had triumphed,
The vile selfishness that had triumphed.

For a link where you can listen to Venezuela's national anthem, "Gloria al bravo pueblo" (Glory to the Brave People), go to www.vgsbooks.com.

Flag

National Anthem

MARÍA CONCHITA ALONSO (b. 1957) Alonso is one of the most successful Venezuelan entertainers in Hollywood. She was born in Cuba but raised in Venezuela. Alonso won several beauty pageants in the 1970s, including Miss Teen World and Miss Venezuela, before becoming a telenovela star and singer. In 1982 she moved to the United States and has appeared in numerous films and television programs.

LUIS APARICIO (b. 1934) Maracaibo-born, Aparicio was a Major League Baseball shortstop for the Chicago White Sox, the Baltimore Orioles, and the Boston Red Sox. His career lasted nearly twenty years (1956–1973), during which he broke numerous American League records. In 1984 his career was capped off by his induction into the Baseball Hall of Fame.

ANDRÉS BELLO (1781–1865) Bello was an influential South American intellectual. The first twenty years of his life were spent in Caracas, where he was born. He lived the remainder of his life in London and Chile, doing work as a writer, translator, and editor. In addition to his writing, Bello was a scholar and educator and held various government positions.

RÓMULO BETANCOURT (1908–1981) Betancourt was one of the most ardent champions of democracy for Venezuela. He was born in Guatiré (Miranda State). He later founded the political party Acción Democrática (AD, Democratic Action)—originally Organización Venezolana—in 1935 and served as Venezuela's president in the 1940s and again in the 1960s. He enacted major agricultural, economic, and social reforms, including universal suffrage (voting rights), during his presidencies.

SIMÓN BOLÍVAR (1783–1830) Caracas-born Bolívar is Venezuela's most beloved hero. Nicknamed El Libertador (the Liberator), he was at the center of the nineteenth-century South American movement for liberation from colonialism. He led rebel forces in many key battles and helped unite parts of South America to form Gran Colombia in 1819. After its collapse, Bolívar's influence quickly diminished, and he was forced to leave Venezuela. Not until years later was he celebrated for his role in Venezuela's independence.

TERESA CARREÑO (1853–1917) Carreño was an internationally known pianist, composer, and teacher. Born in Caracas, Carreño learned to play the piano at age four and became a child prodigy. Her family fled Venezuela in 1862 and moved to New York, where her musical abilities quickly earned her fame.

RÓMULO GALLEGOS (1884–1969) Born in Caracas, Gallegos was a teacher from 1912 to 1930. During this period, he published many novels, including *Doña Bárbara* in 1929, which was interpreted as an attack on the tyranny of Juan Vicente Gómez. Because of his anti-Gómez stance, Gallegos lived in and out of exile from 1931 until his final return to Venezuela in 1958. In 1947 he was president of Venezuela.

FRANCISCO DE MIRANDA (1750–1816) Caracas-born Miranda became a soldier in the Spanish army and fought in the American Revolutionary War and the French Revolution. He later fought to free Venezuela from Spanish colonial domination in the early 1800s. His nickname El Precursor (the Forerunner) gives credit to his early attempts for Venezuelan independence prior to those of Simón Bolívar.

JOSÉ ANTONIO PÁEZ (1790–1873) Páez was a famous leader of the llaneros (Venezuelan cowboys). Born in Acarigua, New Granada, he became Venezuela's first president in 1830. He was instrumental in defeating the Spanish in Venezuela's fight for independence and later led a separatist movement for Venezuela. Páez served as president two more times before going into exile in 1863.

TERESA DE LA PARRA (1889–1936) Parra was Venezuela's most renowned female writer. She was born Ana Teresa Parra Sanojo in Paris but moved with her family to Venezuela when she was young. Her novels and short stories pointed out social inequalities, particularly those faced by women, in a realistic style.

JOSÉ LUÍS RODRÍGUEZ (b. 1943) Rodríguez, or El Puma, is a Venezuelan megastar. Born in Caracas, his career as a singer began in the late 1960s. He later went on to soap opera stardom after appearing in a popular Puerto Rican telenovela. He later moved to Miami, Florida.

IRENE SÁEZ (b. 1961) Sáez is a popular politician who has become a modern-day role model for women in Venezuela. She first came into the public eye when she won the Miss Universe title in 1981. Her popularity won her the elections for mayor of Chacao and for the governor of Nueva Esparta State.

ARTURO USLAR PIETRI (1906–2001) Uslar Pietri was born in Caracas and became one of Venezuela's most significant intellectuals. He was a novelist, historian, cabinet minister, and television commentator. He was a pioneer of the modern short story in Venezuela, and his writings and opinions covered many topics. His novel *Las lanzas coloradas* (*The Red Lances*) about Venezuela's fight for independence from Spain is considered his finest work.

PATRICIA VELASQUEZ (b. 1971) Actress Patricia Velasquez was born in Guajíra and is part Wayúu Indian. Her career began in modeling but has taken off in Hollywood since her debut in the film *The Mummy Returns* and her regular role on the network sitcom *Arrested Development*.

OMAR VIZQUEL (b. 1967) Caracas-born Omar Enrique Vizquel Gonzalez is the shortstop for the Cleveland Indians baseball team. He holds many Major League Baseball records and has won nine Gold Glove awards for the American League. In 2004 he made his 2,000th hit.

CABLE CAR OF MÉRIDA The city of Mérida marks the first stop for the longest and highest *teleférico* (cable car) in the world. Four trams, each carrying up to forty people, ride along a cable wire that stretches nearly 8 miles (12.5 km) from Mérida to Pico Espejo. Riders can take in the sights of the forests and towns below or follow the mountain trails at any of the five stops.

CANAIMA NATIONAL PARK This park, which lies in the Gran Sabana, is one of the largest national parks in the world. Visitors can view the unusual, indigenous plant life that grows on the tops of the tepuís or take a trip to Venezuela's most famous natural wonder—Angel Falls. Located on an upper tributary of the Caroní River, Angel Falls is the highest waterfall in the world, with a total drop of 3,212 feet (979 m).

GUÁCHARO NATURAL CAVE PARK The highlight of this park near Caripe, a town near the northeastern Caribbean city of Cumaná, is the Cave of the Guácharo. The inhabitants of this fantastic cave ecosystem include the nocturnal guácharo bird, or oil bird, and bats. Visitors can also marvel at the stalactite and stalagmite formations inside the cave.

GURÍ DAM Officially named Raúl Leoni Hydroelectric Power Station, this dam is one of the largest in the world. It produces most of the electricity for Venezuela and some of its neighboring countries. The water for the dam comes from the Caroní River, a tributary of the Orinoco River. The dam's architecture features the work of Venezuelan artists Carlos Cruz Díez and Alejandro Otero.

LOS LLANOS The main reason to visit the Llanos is the diverse wildlife, including the capybara—the world's largest rodent. The amazing mammals, birds, reptiles, and fish that inhabit the Llanos vary with the seasons, but the dry season is the best time to visit. Driving is an option, but most people choose to fly into the region and stay at tourist ranches.

MARGARITA ISLAND This Caribbean island offers fantastic weather and duty-free shopping. On land, visitors can admire buildings dating back to the sixteenth century or relax on white, sandy beaches. In the water, visitors can dive for pearls or go windsurfing, snorkeling, scuba diving, surfing, or sailing. La Restinga National Park is home to mangrove trees and thousands of birds.

PUERTO AYACUCHO This city of over eighty thousand people lies along the Orinoco River in the northwestern corner of Amazonas State. Visitors can purchase indigenous crafts and traditional foods at the city's markets. Usually, only scientists and missionaries who have obtained special permission can venture into the heart of the nearby Amazon jungle, so the Museo Ethnológico de Territorio Federal Amazonas (the Ethnological Museum) provides a fascinating alternative for learning about the customs and culture of the indigenous groups who live in the rain forests.

audiencia: an administrative center or seat of government

autopista: a system of superhighways

barrio: the urban area of a Venezuelan city, usually associated with poorer districts

captaincy general: a military governorship

caudillo: a tyrannical political leader with military followers

concession: the right to undertake and profit by a specific activity, such as the right to drill for oil in Venezuela in exchange for a share of the profits

cordillera: a mountain chain. The word *cordillera* comes from the Spanish word for rope, or string.

coup d'état: a sudden, violent overthrow of an existing government by a small group

criollo: a Venezuela-born descendant of the Spanish. Also called a Creole.

delta: a low triangular area of land where a river divides before entering a larger body of water

gross domestic product (GDP): a measure of the total value of goods and services produced within a country in a year. A similar measurement is gross national product (GNP). GDP and GNP are often measured in terms of purchasing power parity (PPP). PPP converts values to international dollars, making it possible to compare how much similar goods and services cost to the residents of different countries.

indigenous: native to a specific country. Indigenous peoples of Venezuela include the Wayúu, the Warao, the Yanomami, and the Pemón.

junta: a council that gains power after a revolution

mestizo: a person of mixed racial ancestry. In Venezuela mestizos usually have some combination of Indian, Spanish, and African backgrounds.

nationalize: to convert from private to government ownership and control

PDVSA: Petróleos de Venezuela, S.A., is Venezuela's government-run oil company

rancho: a makeshift housing development on the outskirts of an urban area. The poorer citizens living in ranchos often live without proper water, sewage, and electrical services.

referendum: a direct vote by the people to approve or reject legislation (laws)

refinery: an industrial plant used for purifying or processing raw materials

telenovela: a Spanish-language soap opera

tepuí: a flat-topped mountain found in the Guiana Highlands region of Venezuela

tributary: a stream or river that flows into a larger stream, river, or lake

Baynham, Angela. *Insight Guide: Venezuela.* Rev. ed. Singapore: Apa Publications GmbH & Co., 2002.
This comprehensive look at the history, people, and places of Venezuela includes full-color photos on every page as well as countless maps and travel tips. Although this book was written with travelers in mind, researchers will find that all the chapters hold useful insights into Venezuelan culture.

Bureau of Western Hemisphere Affairs. "Venezuela." *U.S. Department of State.* November 2003.
<http://state.gov/r/pa/ei/bgn/1859.htm> (June 15, 2004).
"Background Note: Venezuela" contains updated facts from the Bureau of Western Hemisphere Affairs covering Venezuela's geography, people, government, and economy. Heavier coverage is given to Venezuela's people and history, current government, national security, political conditions, economy, and foreign relations. The site also includes important contact information for travelers to Venezuela.

Dinneen, Mark. *Culture and Customs of Venezuela.* Westport, CT: Greenwood Press, 2001.
An excellent reference for all things cultural. Each chapter provides a thorough history of a different aspect of Venezuelan culture—including religion, social customs, broadcasting and print media, cinema, literature, performing arts, and art and architecture. References and further reading are provided at the end of each relevant chapter. The back matter includes a glossary of terms frequently encountered in researching Venezuela.

Economist.com. 2004.
<http://economist.com> (June 15, 2004).
The *Economist*'s website contains articles on the current economic, political, and social situation in Venezuela.

The Europa World Yearbook, 2003. London: Europa Publications Limited, 2002.
This annual publication contains a detailed survey of Venezuela's recent history, government, defense, economic affairs, social welfare, and education. A statistical survey and directory follows and includes information on areas such as the constitution, political organizations, judicial system, religion, media, trade, transport, and tourism.

Food and Agriculture Organization of the United Nations. *FAOSTAT Homepage.* 2004.
<http://apps.fao.org/default.jsp> (June 15, 2004).
Agricultural, fishing, and forestry statistics from the Food and Agriculture Organization (FAO) of the United Nations can be found on this site.

Haggerty, Richard A., ed. *Venezuela: A Country Study.* 4th ed. Washington, D.C.: Library of Congress, 1993.
The U.S. Department of the Army prepared books in this series to educate the public about lesser-known countries. The book contains a profile of Venezuela and has chapters on its historical setting, society and its environment, economy, government and politics, and national security.

LatinFocus. "Venezuela." *LatinFocus Consensus Forecast.* **2004.**
<http://www.latin-focus.com/latinfocus/countries/venezuela/venezuela.htm>
(June 15, 2004).
LatinFocus aims to provide up-to-date economic and financial information on
Latin American countries. Links to the latest news stories and general infor-
mation on each country are also available.

Lombardi, John V. *Venezuela: The Search for Order, the Dream of*
Progress. **New York: Oxford University Press, 1982.**
The author provides a detailed history of Venezuela, including a political
chronology. The land section of the book includes separate maps for each of
the geographical regions of the country.

Murphy, Alan. *Venezuela Handbook.* **Bath, UK: Footprint**
Handbooks Ltd., 1998.
This travel guidebook gives a firsthand account of the geography, history, peo-
ple, culture, and sites of Venezuela.

Population Reference Bureau. **2003.**
<http://www.prb.org> (June 15, 2004).
The annually updated statistics on this site provide an excellent source of
demographic information for Venezuela and other countries, on everything
from birthrates and death rates, to the infant mortality rate, and the percentage of the population with HIV/AIDS. Check out the March 2003 article
"Population Dynamics in Latin America" for an overview of the entire region.

U.S. Department of Energy. "Venezuela." *Energy Information*
Administration: Monthly Energy Review. **May 27, 2004.**
<http://www.eia.doe.gov/emeu/mer/contents.html> (June 15, 2004).
This site contains detailed information on Venezuela's oil, natural gas, and
hydroelectricity industries. Links and further resources are given.

Webster, Donovan. "The Orinoco: Into the Heart of Venezuela."
National Geographic Magazine, **April 1998, 2–31.**
The author travels the course of the Orinoco River from its source to its delta
and shares his perceptions of the people, wildlife, and landscape along the way.
Brief historical information is also provided, but the main feature of the arti-
cle is the photography.

Further Reading and Websites

BBC Country Profile: Venezuela
<http://news.bbc.co.uk/1/hi/world/americas/country_profiles/1229345.stm>
Learn about Venezuela's current political situation from this BBC News website, which includes profiles of Venezuela's leaders and background information on the media.

Caracas News
<http://www.caracasnews.com/>
Read current news stories about Venezuela and other South American countries. The site covers business, politics, economy, sports, and science news. It also includes links to other Venezuela sites and on-line news sources, including the World News Network.

Embassy of the Bolivarian Republic of Venezuela in the United States of America
<http://www.embavenez-us.org>
Read information on the government, economy, business, culture, and tourism from Venezuela's embassy in Washington, D.C.

George, Uwe. "Venezuela's Islands in Time," *National Geographic Magazine*, May 1989, 526–561.
This article is full of excellent information on the geological formation and unique ecosystems of the tepuís in the Gran Sabana. The author gives a first-hand account of the region. Full-color photographs, maps, and diagrams are featured.

Hamilton, Dominic. *Traveler's Venezuela Companion*. Guilford, CT: The Globe Pequot Press, 2001.
<http://www.venezuelavoyage.com/index.htm>
Photographs, maps, and text describe the history, people, culture, and landscape of the regions of Venezuela. An equally good accompanying website is maintained by the author and contains additional information, including video footage.

Nott, David. *Angels Four*. Englewood Cliffs, NJ: Prentice-Hall, 1972.
This novel is a first-person account of the first four men to reach the top of Angel Falls, in 1971.

Tahan, Raya. *The Yanomami of South America*. Minneapolis: Lerner Publications Company, 2002.
Colorful layout and photos accentuate this introduction to the Yanomami peoples of Venezuela and Brazil. Readers will learn about the environment of the Amazon jungle, which the Yanomami call home, as well as the history, culture, and lifestyles of these people. A glossary and recommended books, videos, websites, and organizations are included in the back matter.

Think-Venezuela.net
<http://www.think-venezuela.net/food.htm>
Check out this on-line tourism directory for extensive information about Venezuela's money and costs, security, communication, holidays, health care, attractions, and weather. Most sections have photos, maps, and links.

Venezuela Yours (Venezuela Tuya)
<http://www.venezuelatuya.com/eng.htm>
This colorful and user-friendly site has basic information about Venezuela and photographs of the landscape and people. The text is also available in other languages, including Spanish.

vgsbooks.com
<http:www.vgsbooks.com>
Visit vgsbooks.com, the home page of the Visual Geography Series®, which is updated regularly. You can get linked to all sorts of useful on-line information, including websites on the geography, history, demographics, culture, and economics of Venezuela and many other countries. The vgsbooks.com site is also a great resource for late-breaking news and statistics.

Willis, Terry. *Venezuela: Enchantment of the World.* New York: Children's Press, Scholastic Inc., 2003.
Intended for young adults, this book is an excellent introduction to the geography, history, people, and culture of Venezuela. The chapters on Venezuela's plants and animals, culture, and daily life are particularly useful.

Index

Captions for photos appearing on cover and chapter openers:

Cover: Angel Falls, Venezuela's top tourist attraction, is named after Jimmy Angel, a U.S. pilot who discovered the falls in 1935.

pp. 4–5 Mount Roraima, the largest of the flat-topped tepuís at 9,094 feet (2,772 m), rises high above the cloud cover near Venezuela's border with Guyana and Brazil. Wild tales of Roraima's unique plant and animal life are believed to have inspired Sir Arthur Conan Doyle's novel *The Lost World*, a title that is often applied to the tepuí region itself.

pp. 8–9 The isolated Llanos, or plains, of Venezuela stretch for miles, accounting for nearly one-third of Venezuela's total area.

pp. 22–23 Citizens of Venezuela participated in the Mega March on December 14, 2002, to protest the Chávez government. An estimated 2.5 million people took part in the march.

pp. 36–37 In Caracas, a group of boys waits outside their public school for violin lessons to begin.

pp. 44–45 Venezuelans participate in the dance of *los diablos* (the devil) during a Corpus Christi festival. Participants in the dance wear masks with many different horns on them. Each horn symbolizes a sin for which the wearer will ask forgiveness.

pp. 56–57 An oil storage platform sits on the surface of Lake Maracaibo. Despite the presence of so much oil, Venezuela still relies on fishing in the lake as a source of income.

Photo Acknowledgments

The images in this book are used with the permission of: © Silva/UNEP/Peter Arnold, Inc., pp. 4–5; © Ron Bell/Digital Cartographics, pp. 6, 11; © Gabriela Medina/SuperStock, pp. 8–9; © Jorge Silva/Reuters/CORBIS, p. 10; © Victor Englebert, pp. 13, 36–37; © Carlos Adolfo Sastoque N./SuperStock, p. 15; © Kevin Schafer/Peter Arnold, Inc., p. 16; © Sergio Pitamitz/SuperStock, p. 17; © John Kreul Collection/Independent Picture Service, pp. 18, 54, 60; © Julio Etchart/Peter Arnold, Inc., p. 19; © SuperStock, pp. 20–21, 55; © Luciano Borsari/ZUMA Press, pp. 22–23, 39; Library of Congress, pp. 27 [LC-USZ62-074786], 28 [LC-USZ62-80182]; © Bettmann/CORBIS, pp. 32, 48; © Reuters/CORBIS, pp. 34, 44–45; © Sergi Reboredo/Peter Arnold, Inc., p. 38; © Pablo Corral V/CORBIS, pp. 41, 52; Pan American Health Organization, p. 42; Art Museum of the Americas, Organization of American States, p. 46; © Oscar Sabetta/Getty Images, p. 50; © Joseph Fabry/Time Life Pictures/Getty Images, p. 51; © Yann Arthus-Bertrand/CORBIS, pp. 56–57; © B. Swanson/Art Directors, pp. 62–63; © Kimberly White/Getty Images, p. 64; Banknotes.com, p. 68; Laura Westlund, p. 69.

Cover: © S. Mead/Art Directors. Back cover: NASA